THE SOUND OF HER VOICE

The Sound of Her Voice

A memoir
by

SARA GELBARD

Adelaide Books
New York / Lisbon
2020

THE SOUND OF HER VOICE
A memoir
By Sara Gelbard

Published by Adelaide Books, New York / Lisbon
adelaidebooks.org
Editor-in-Chief
Stevan V. Nikolic

For any information, please address Adelaide Books
at info@adelaidebooks.org
or write to:
Adelaide Books
244 Fifth Ave. Suite D27
New York, NY, 10001

ISBN: 978-1-952570-19-3

Printed in the United States of America

Contents

Let's look for secret places
Somewhere in the world
On the blue shores of silence.
Or where the storm has passed…

— Pablo Neruda

The Sound of Her Voice

When I reached the age of 70, I got to the point where she could finally tell her story. She couldn't tell it before. I had just begun spending more time with my husband in Punta del Este in Uruguay, an elegant town by the sea, with a pure and stunning quiet, and the most luminous sunsets and sunrises. The beauty of Punta with its beaches, and the embracing and healing sea surrounding both sides of the town, somehow made her bubble up. She saw the water and she came out. It couldn't be on the corner of Tenth Street and Greenwich Avenue in New York, where I also live and work. It is too crowded there, too noisy. I never had time for her there.

One day in Punta, she just started talking. Was she talking before and no one would listen or did she never have a voice? I believe her voice was always there. But I was too busy managing my real estate business, being with my husband, Carlos, and traveling back and forth to Israel to see my family. I was too busy seeing friends, and learning, and pushing myself, as people in New York do. She had to be safe to tell her story since her soul, her little self, had only known danger. If she revealed herself before, if she came out and was herself and spoke her mind, she had to pay a price. Annihilation. Being ostracized. Being thrown out on her own with no one to support her. She had to be sure I could hear her before she would speak.

Each morning in Punta, I began going to Boca Chica, a café near my house to hear her. I went after I had walked the dog in the very early morning, our ritual, which I feel is a sacramental activity together, as does the dog by the way since he so attentively wakes me to begin. I bring him back home and have a coffee there, I take my notebooks and pencils and unfortunately my phone. I am still in business in New York, even living in Punta, and the waitress knows me, and her, and brings me a cortado, and I try to begin.

It is hard to be a beginner and exciting at the same time. Strange how hard it is to hear one's own "still small voice" within. There are so many voices talking to us, demanding of us, so many sounds and noises.

I hear music in the background as I start to write. The place does not have a view which I think will help me. Gila, my writing coach, said to write 3 to 5 pages a day, and she thought I should write in English. I think so, too. My family is on my mind because, if it is in English, I am not sure they will be able to read this. But I also think writing in English provides me the necessary distance to tell this story.

As I begin, I have just come back from Israel where I was born, on a kibbutz. I am shocked how estranged I feel from my country, I am no longer part of that culture. However, I don't feel estranged when I am with my brother, David. On that visit, we traveled a day in the Galil and drove through the magical green hills of our childhood. When we were children, there were never places to stop for coffee, but now we stopped in a place on the Adir mountain overlooking the other mountains at the border of Lebanon, a typical Galil vista, where so many homes and towns are hidden. Then to Kadem and a Druze village, Chorphish, on the hillside.

We stopped to eat food that I had never eaten before, as usual dirt cheap, but so good. I love the food in Israel, its freshness, simplicity. I have never liked French cooking, it's too fancy and complicated. One area where Arabs and Jews are integrated in Israel is food. We took so much from the Arab culture and it is truly a part of our Israeli cuisine.

We kept on driving in our majestic Galil. It was a day to remember. My brother and I did not live as a family when we were children in the kibbutz. We hardly saw each other or our parents. Now I make a point to strengthen my family ties with my siblings. On this trip to Israel, I also saw my sister, Elana, whom I find I always want to care for and protect. I know she did not have protection in the kibbutz' Children's House that each of us grew up in. Not that I had much protection myself as a child. But this is why I know what she feels, even perhaps if she does not.

I am the oldest and, when I was born, my mother was thrilled to have a child. My father travelled a lot, leaving the kibbutz, helping the dispersed Jews in Europe come to Israel. Ecstatic as my mother was with her firstborn, she was only allowed twenty-minute feeding visits to the Children's House. Then she had to leave no matter how I screamed for her. And she would hear me scream in my loneliness and fear as she walked by the Children's House, but the rules were stringent: Leave the child alone. Do not go to her no matter how much she cries to be held. It was painful for my mother. Never mind for me. For me it was terrifying and excruciating. It was a form of torture. What they do to prisoners, they put them in solitary confinement with limited contact with their loved ones. And yet, my mother loved me. She just had to sneak that love in, in the intervals where she was allowed to, a visitor to an inmate. And then leave me alone as a baby and infant, sobbing my heart out not to be left in the dark there.

My parents felt, in their hearts, it was against human nature to have such arbitrary separation between parents and children. They knew, but it was the rules and they were good kibbutzniks.

My father tried to humanize the experience. For instance, he brought live animals into the kibbutz to help create a little zoo for the children and he brought clothing and many gifts back from his travels.

My mother also had her misgivings about the stringencies of life in the Children's House, but she insisted that the family stay, no matter what. She had made a moral commitment to be part of it.

Each of us children in my family experienced the Children's House differently. My sister Elana, five years younger than me, was born to a different mother than me, one who was more beaten down by life at the kibbutz, so she was more than willing to give the caring and responsibility of a child to the metapelet in the Children's House. With me, she may have had more conflict complying with the rules.

For me, the Children's House was a great form of sadness and isolation but, for Elana, it actually was a home. I admit that Elana's classmates were unusually kind and she still gets together every month with some of her classmates, now that they are retired. David, my brother, the youngest, also had a class of loving children. In both their classes, there were cases of polio and the whole class was quarantined and the other children nurtured the children with polio. Elana's class is still supporting the girl who had polio. And, in David's class, a child with a severe case of polio, ended up marrying and having a family.

In my case, we were not such a homogenous group. I was among 7 girls and 14 boys, and there was much cruelty in the early, first kibbutz system. The philosophy was at its strictest and all that mattered was the kibbutz. We were not to have personal feelings and we were not to be coddled. I remember, in later years, when we were joining the army, telling my teacher that one of my classmates was unprepared and he was going to fall apart in the army. But no one at that time in the kibbutz system made room for special needs. The system did not pay attention to anything that was out of the norm. We were all to be strong Jews, no matter the reality of our nature. (The boy I warned about did fall apart in the army and ended up committing suicide later.) Even after many years had passed, when our kibbutz began to pay more attention to children's needs, and now considered that children sleeping in their parent's home is important, one of my classmates fought against it. She was hanging onto the rigidity of the past. The move to change was passed, however. My brother's children, who lived with he and his wife on the kibbutz, slept at home.

A deep sadness is rising to the surface as I write. When I first came to New York as a young woman, when I essentially ran away, Preston, a spiritual psychoanalyst who affected my life deeply and of whom I will speak often, when he first met me, said, "I see a million tears in your eyes that you need to cry from your childhood." Who would dare to cry in the Children's Houses where we were all supposed to be little soldiers, where we were all supposed to love this communal living of rules and duties and no love or nurturing? To show unhappiness or sadness meant there was something wrong with you. You were not a good kibbutznik, you were not strong enough. We in the kibbutz were part of something big: building Israel, a most righteous society. We didn't have much, but it belonged to everybody. We lived on ideology. And to express vulnerability was considered weakness.

But Preston was right: I was born to cry, I have that type of nature, and I had to suppress it. But those feelings are close to the surface now, I see, as I pick up my pen and the water of the sea surrounds me on both sides and wells up inside me.

This coffeeshop is not perfect in that it can be noisy, sometimes the music is loud, but it's a place I can hear my voice, her voice, the child no one knew. There was beautiful music at home this morning that Carlos had on, that helped me to feel my grief, but I do not want to write at home. Carlos has his desk; I don't have my corner. Maybe we should look for it.

It is the next morning and I am walking my dog, the most special part of my day, seeing his beautiful black silhouette, galloping against the silver sea. It is just us and it is heaven. Even when it rains and the wind is blowing, it is us, the sea and the sky. That shared solitary moment. In the afternoon, when the sun came out, I took a photo of our terrace overlooking the sea and the sky. A simple snap on my iphone and it made me happy and I shared it with a lot of people. The sea strengthens and softens me, its power and beauty, and the sun at this time of the day does also, when it is ready to set.

Yet, as I write today, I don't feel completely inside my heart. My little manager inside me is trying to take over with a list of things to do and I am trying to quiet him down. He is always first in the morning dictating the activities of the day. No more! First quiet, listening, writing, then organizing.

I wish this world was made up of less words. It is my husband Carlos' best quality, few words. It is cold today in the café, even with the sun shining. And here I am trying to write and my manager coming in the back door, talking, when I take this time for myself. We should be doing this, be doing that, he tells me!

I look around this coffeeshop and see families communicating, children laughing and playing with their toys. And I remember that the only thing that was mine in a room of 4 children was a Renoir print of 2 girls playing the piano. My mother had put it up on the wall. In doing so, she wanted to warm up the bare walls that were empty, where nothing could give warmth and comfort. Other than that, our room in the Children's House was stark, without toys, no transitional objects. Could we children give each other a sense of security and warmth? At night, there was only one woman circulating between the Children's Houses. And how many hours of lying all alone until she came? What were the kibbutz leaders thinking when they came up with this system of leaving children without any sense of home and security all by themselves in empty rooms? Was this the response to the submissiveness of the Jews in the Holocaust? Was Sparta what we were emulating?

The Children's House was a t-shape, concrete, one story building. You came into the hall and then to the right was the dining room and a classroom. The showers and the cupboards for our clothes were opposite to the dining room (which created a square). In the middle across from the hallway was a row of six bedrooms with a common hallway. We only left the building to go to work and to visit our parents in the afternoon. Everything we needed to do to live, such as eating and sleeping and studying, was in the one-story concrete building. We all wore the same clothes, pants and shirts.

It is empty here today in Boca Chica. I have such love for empty places, empty beaches, after having been forced to live with others all my life. A place to just be. Amy Winehouse is singing, and I feel such sadness, life cut short. I think I am trying to stay away from my manager, this manager who keeps me in line. He has been with me a long time, my companion and my guard and my parent. Preston said we had to be our own guard in the kibbutz, our own guard telling us we should get up, go do this duty, complete that. Don't go to your parent's house when you are scared. No crying. No getting out of step. I don't think my inner manager and I ever had a friendship, we just worked together. I also call him "the organizer." I don't remember if we had conversations when I was a child. Did he protect me at night? I don't think so. He was scared too. I don't think he was consoling me. Maybe he didn't have the words. They didn't exist. We lived in a land of strict activities, a desert of emotion, not a world of language and exploration of feelings. The organizer had a very definite role, he kept me going, he kept my responsibilities in line. He woke me up in the morning. And I needed him so much because I had an inner conflict, sadness and rebellion at being so structured and not allowed to feel and come to know my inner self. If not for him, I would have just stopped. But because of him, I excelled. This busyness and drive that my manager insisted on kept me from feeling pain, even though he bossed me around.

In truth, my manager never let me down throughout my entire life. My manager was the parent inculcated inside me. The most succinct experience that I had with him was when I was getting divorced from my first husband. I never thought I would divorce. I did not want more separation, more withdrawal of love. I did not think I could live through it again. I remember leaving a bar mitzvah celebration with my then husband, hoping against hope he would stay with me that afternoon, even after I knew he wanted to separate. We had left the event as a couple, but he immediately went to his car and took off, leaving me standing there lost and abandoned.

My heart almost jumped out of my chest. My little girl went hiding, sobbing in the corner. My hope of having an afternoon together with him melted, evaporated, leaving no trace. Now it was just she and of course him (the manager), and me. When we got home, she was running back and forth from one side of the apartment, disheveled, restless. I didn't know what to do but the little organizer quietly came up with the idea to take a walk in the park. He thought the little one would stop running and calm down since talking to her was impossible. And so we went on a very long walk, the three of us. It was cold, the sun slowly setting down, and my little one got tired and slowed down as well. But the sunlight cheered her up and brought her hope.

Shortly after my first husband left, I had to register for my class at Fordham. I had been so despondent that I thought I could not move but my manager would hear nothing of it. He got me up and out and had me register and kept me on track. I don't remember him yelling at me or being impatient. As active as he was, he also knew when to wait.

He and my mother were aligned in their focus on work. It was her mantra that, when distraught, "perform." She was a first-grade teacher and specialized in working with children who had difficulties with math and reading. She took her position and work very seriously. Years later when she heard a teaching class given on the radio that she thought might help me in my own teaching, she wrote down the whole program for me word by word. Work was the kibbutz mantra as well, but not everyone obeyed it.

I feel in this writing I want to listen to what he would not listen to, the voice inside. My manager lived outside, in the world. It takes a real deep listening to listen to the deeper voice he was unable to hear.

My little one is also listening, and I am trying to listen to her, but it is hard, her voice right now is tentative. This child was so beautiful. I suppose she was born like that, happy, with a very sad mother, a mother with a grieving heart. Even though my mother was joyous when I was first born, she still felt guilty about the burning house she left behind in Poland. She never told us the story about her family. The little bit of information I heard was from a friend of my mother's who was from her hometown and also lived on the kibbutz. My mother held onto the friendship with that woman for dear life, a lifeline to her past although my father kept a distance from her. Even though my mother's voice was beautiful, she never sang in the choir; she could not sing with her survivor's guilt. She sewed and crocheted exquisitely and made her profession an art. Her work was her refuge. She told me,"All my problems disappear when I go to work. It is the best therapy." And, indeed, she is right. It has been my refuge, my joy and sorrow as well. In my field of real estate sales, believe me, one has plenty of joys and sorrows.

My manager has become more benign, I notice, now that we have been together 70 years. But he has worked hard. I was a leader in the youth movement in the kibbutz, an officer in the navy, then came to New York with $500 in my pocket, got a degree in economics, built a successful business. I have things to show for having this guard live inside me. But I could not stay deaf to her and a part of me crying all the time. The outside versus the inside. It is she who decided that if we write about it, those tears will have their voice and expression. It is our road to healing.

I think what I really want to write about is the emotional journey of the past. At what cost it took to get to where I am now. Other writers, like Amos Oz, describe exquisitely the dynamics and the shape of the communal life in the kibbutz. But I want to portray the nuance of having to perform like an automaton and the loneliness of that struggle. Someone told me recently they would not have known I needed help and support in those years. We didn't learn to show our feelings, we demanded of ourselves constant activity.

Soon I will be back in New York and I also have my place there to cry, if I need to. It does not come easily to me. I need music or sad movies to access my pain, or writing in Punta. I can feel it here because Carlos is so natural at "being alone together," Winnicott's expression for the mother being in the kitchen and the child has the security to explore and learn on her own. Carlos understands and respects the space between us. One of the reasons we are together is his interior life which is a huge value to me and how he is always there. I did not have someone steady, caring for me, while I was growing up in the kibbutz. Many children were around me but there were no patient adults being loving as we explored. They did not have time for it, they were busy fulfilling their own duties. The moment the kibbutz philosophy intervened in the mother/child relationship, the whole concept of "being alone together" was abandoned. What we had instead was each of us growing up along side each other, everyone doing the same thing. We did not have the ability to individualize on any level. Preston said that solitude and the interior life was not on the map in the kibbutz. He is right. We were busy little soldiers, doing.

Carlos helps me rebuild; he is in the background where I can leave the shore and explore my emotions safely. The poet Rilke wrote, "…a good marriage is one in which each partner appoints the other to be the guardian of his solitude," the place where we each guard what is most difficult and precious in each other.

Carlos was my first real home. I did not marry a man who supported me financially or who was the caretaker in that way. I was perfectly capable of doing that for myself. I chose a man who could provide an emotional home for me, which is what I desperately needed. He does such an important thing for me by being, not doing. I'd had enough of "doing."

I chose a man for what I could feel with him, rather than how he would take care of my financial needs, and Preston said, "You're very lucky you saw money for what it is." I understood him to mean that I did not give it more importance than emotional connection. Preston felt it was my mother who instilled the positive values of the kibbutz, where money is not a highest value. Yes, yes we need it and it offers freedom and an ability to choose but it is not the reason for being. And for me, I never confused it for home. It is connection that is home.

He is on shore
My solid backing
As I go out exploring.

Today is another morning and I took another walk to the beach, this one windy and rainy, with my dog. These are most wondrous moments. Us alone in nature. Aloneness not loneliness.

Now I sit here with my pen and my organizer is up so much earlier than me and he has already started with his planning. I have to listen very intently to hear what it is she needs. When did she lose her voice? I see her in my mind kissing her doll at my 5th birthday, happy, no sister born yet, my parents all to myself in Rome, where my father took us when he was working there. Then an abrupt change, which felt like an earthquake: the return to the kibbutz, giving up all her private possessions to the group. Her own first dress, blue, gathered in front with white and red threads… it was the piece of clothing she loved. But that dress became part of the communal clothes we children wore when we went to visit the city. And my bicycle, everyone riding it in intervals of 15 minutes so it was no longer mine but theirs! No one ever asked her if she was okay sharing her bike and new dress. It was not okay, we felt robbed. All that was hers was no more in a second, when we returned from Italy, and no father or mother now, no one to console and explain.

I can just imagine how she felt, crushed to lose everything at once, her parents, her private possessions, and back to the Children's House after experiencing living at home with her parents in Italy. Back to the 24 children with one teacher and a metapelet.

No wonder she became silent. She stopped talking. Not sure for how many years. "It was a real crisis," my mother said later.

But this did not stop her from living by her rules. I remember when I was older, I bought my mother a ceramic dish, like a basket, not something useful, a gift, a surprise. I had to go to the city to get it, and she said, "Sara, next time do not buy something without a use." And she did not receive the gift. She did not realize I needed her sensitivity, to be loved for my self expression in a system that repressed self expression.

But she had her story too, a story she never told. When she was nineteen, she left her family in Poland, and joined the Zionist youth movement, and with a lot of hardship, she got to the shores of Israel and the kibbutz. It became her new home after her whole family were killed in the War. She would not risk losing this home for the world, even if she had to leave her baby screaming for her at the top of her lungs. How much she must have suffered to sacrifice her maternal feelings for the kibbutz, for this country asking for the ultimate sacrifices.

They were taught these sacrifices were needed for Israel's survival. I suppose I am a part of the second generation whose parents paid a heavy price to leave their familes and homeland to come to Israel. But we children of these parents paid a price, as well. We paid the price for our parent's broken hearts and our hearts that broke because of them. My mother's heart had been shut closed when she realized the fate of her family in Poland. There was no opening for light or healing. Her heart was in the middle of her body in a black box of grief, without keys. I looked for the keys to her heart all my life, to bring light to her, without success. Yes, the kibbutz was a good option, it helped her to bear children, and the kibbutz helped her bring them up. With her heavy heart, she couldn't do it alone. And she subscribed wholeheartedly to a society that didn't emphasize individual needs. A society that worked to change the intellectual book-worm Jew into a new Jew, built of values of mostly physical prowess and hard work. These new Jews would now be able to protect themselves, and it made sense since resources in Israel then were scarce and everyone had to pull together to build a land.

As separated as we were, I also realize now, my mother and I were soul mates in some ways. She wrote poetry, had a strong work ethic, as I do and, because of that, my body felt her pain as mine. Preston said that I now seek this special relationship of soul mate with other people to repeat what I had with her.

When my mother died, on my first visit back I went to her grave. I had an overwhelming feeling that she was joyous to finally be reunited with her family that she lost. She died at 70, my age now, and here I am starting to take stock of my life. Hopefully I will wander through my own grief with an open heart. I think it is my mother who is near to me today, not my little one. And my old companion – the manager. He is a total surprise; I never thought about him before the book and he is so much a part of my life.

In my loneliness as a child, I felt I was in the desert with no one to talk to about my real feelings. It took 40 years in the desert for Moses and the Jews to get to the promised land. Almost as long for me. No wonder my manager is trying to keep things going.

My first freedom from the kibbutz loneliness was, of all things, the army. I remember the day, the happiness, the exhilaration, when going to the first training. Now I was free to make my own mistakes and live on my own terms, not those of the kibbutz. Most people don't think of the army as a place of freedom but at least you could make some choices of your own. You could be an individual doing the expected activities.

We army recruits had to congregate in Haifa, where they provided transportation to where we would be inducted, and begin six weeks of basic training. I felt much easier than in the kibbutz. It wasn't so loaded. It did not carry as much sorrow. I was soon stationed in the navy, had an interesting job in a bunker, monitoring communications with a submarine.

As I sit here writing, I worry if I am able to do this, tell this story. I spoke to Rachel and she helped me, telling me that Preston said if one speaks well, one can write well. I know that using the right words in real estate has helped me, choosing the right words to describe a home, and in the process of negotiation, it makes all the difference. Rachel said that when you write, you become your own friend. I feel much less need for company. My writing is internal and not something I need to discuss.

Back to the army. Part of me was such a performing good soldier, silently hiding my suffering. Like my mother, I see.

We were regimented into a routine in the army, and we kibbutzim young people were accustomed to doing well with that and to managing physical expectations. And maybe because of this, I was asked to enlist in the Officers Course. But of course, in the army one is also exposed to situations that are of real danger.

I remember in the Officer's training, we practiced with simulated hand grenades. One had to take the pin out of the hand grenade and be sure to throw it in a circular upward motion, as far away from yourself as you could because, if it landed the wrong way, it could explode and injure you. Soon, we were having practice with a live hand grenade. We were all anxious and afraid of it, even with an officer by our side. One of the cadets threw it the wrong way and, almost instantly, a piece went to her heart, and she died. She was in my bunker. I knew her well. After the accident, they canceled everything. We left the practice, which was far away from our camp, and went back. It was such a tragedy.

They summoned the highest-ranking Israeli woman officer in charge of overseeing all the women soldiers in the army and navy to come and speak to us female officers-in-training. I was selected to greet and salute her. We were all so shaken up and, when I raised my hand in salute and repeated the traditional phrase we stated in this ritual, she said, "You are speaking too low. Can you speak louder?" My voice was trembling.

My friend was given a military funeral and gun salute when we buried her, but to see her parents was unbearable. I used to see them come to the gates to bring her packages of cookies and sweets which she shared with us when we were training. They were so loving to her.

Even with all the terrible sad things we saw in training, I had a sense of pride when I graduated. The cousin of one of the women in my bunker was the head of the Israeli Air Force, a revered position, and he came to visit us prior to graduating. It was a great honor. We had a graduation book and one of my friends wrote of me, "You have such rolling laughter and joy and such sadness." So seemingly, even though I had done well as I did in the kibbutz, my little one did rear her little head. But she still had not been heard. Not till now.

In the navy as I was ending my service, they approached me to stay on with them, since I was an officer. "Would you sign with us?" the higher command asked. I did and I was ready to make it a career since I thought it a stepping stone to leaving the kibbutz. However, my parents strongly objected; they did not want me leaving the kibbutz, and I had to reneg on my signing. I went back to the kibbutz and, after a year, I chose to begin a two-year program for study of dance and movement in a College in Tel Aviv.

After I completed my studies, I started teaching elementary high school and college level dance and movement in a college in the desert in Sde Boker, where Ben Gurion settled at the end of his life. (The reason he settled there is he wanted to set an example for people to move to more challenging places than the cities.) My cousin was living there, and she introduced me to this place, and I ended up getting a job there which gave me great experience. It was a wonderful teaching opportunity, and a bit like a kibbutz setting, and there were special features of this community that I was attracted to. There was a group there from the States, intelligent and interesting, and they invited me to their gatherings every Friday nght, and I began to see that could pave the way to my possibly getting even further away, to New York.

The setting was a place of arid beauty, inspiring, and the whole group of people were cultured, worldly and sophisticated, and a window into a different life for me. One man was from Chicago, and he was one of my neighbors in the communal housing, and he fell in love with me. I totally rejected him, but he waited patiently for me and eventually we became involved.

On my 25th birthday, the sun was about to go down beyond the dunes, and my parents arrived on the last bus with dire faces. It turned out they were there on a mission to find out if I was having an affair. We spent a few hours together in the late afternoon after the sunset, and a friend in the group showed up and invited me and my friend from Chicago to the next Friday dinner. My parents got their proof. Unbeknownest to me, they went to my cousin to discuss it, and asked her how could she allow this? After they left, my cousin let me know of my parents 'interrogation,' and I sank into a deep depression. I felt violated. Being excellent soldiers of the kibbutz, they had not been there to hold, comfort or protect me all my life. After a life of struggles and accomplishment, being in the service, college and now a working life, now they choose to come to supervise me? And through the back door. They were claiming all the rights of parents without having been parents. They had not earned that right, I thought.

In my hurt, I proceded to get a big boil on my face, my steps became heavy, and the air around me felt still and quiet, as before a storm. Days, weeks went by, and then I knew. I could not repeat this experience. I have to leave, I decided. This would be the last birthday we celebrate together. I am leaving Israel, I told myself, and going to stay in New York and create a new life, the life I should have, not the one I am living and, there, I will heal my past. Since many of the people in the community were from the United States, they helped me to take this big step and it was not that difficult to arrange.

I applied for a student visa from the Martha Graham School of Dance. I would need to take one class a day for an hour and a half, either in the morning or afternoon, when I got to New York.

I went to Bersheva, the nearest town to Sde Boker, and applied for a passport. I remember it as if was today. There was something so alive about it, I was making a new beginning, something I had never done. At that time, Israel was still drunk on the Six Day war victory; it was a time of hope and pride. Going to the US was not considered an escape. The victory was a huge humiliation to our enemies and ended up, as we all know, not bringing us closer to peace. It complicated the landscape with very complex issues, such as the settlements which are eating us up alive to this day. Who would know we were drunk with the taste and smell of victory? Against this background, I made my plans.

With an overnight stop in Paris, I would arrive in New York in the afternoon and meet my cousin, Ray, who would wait for me in the crowded JFK airport with a white handkerchief.

Just before I left, I was introduced to Rachel, who was to be my closest and best lifelong friend. Rachel is also an Israeli, and she was already living in New York. She said, "I think I read that children from the kibbutzim make the best soldiers in Israel?"

"When you are in an army camp 20 years, it makes sense you would become a great soldier."

Rachel was stunned.

"And furthermore," I added, "other people from other places make just as good soldiers."

I was essentially telling her the Kibbutz was an idealized phenomenon at that time.

She said, "Here is my phone number. Look me up when you come to New York City."

This conversation took place in 1969, just after the Six Day War, and no one spoke critically of Israel. I am sure this is what struck her. Now I had one contact waiting for me.

My parents went with me to the airport to say goodbye. We discussed nothing, none of the reality of this momentous decision I'd made. We were silent about it and kissed goodbye, and I got on the plane. In retrospect, we did not know how to separate better. I was angry and they were overwhelmed. We were to repeat over and over again this loaded silence.

But it makes sense for those who lived through the Holocaust to not know how to separate. They had only known being ripped away. But I did not know that then. I only knew the silence between us.

I remember there were American people on the plane from the same building as my cousin, Ray. They complained about the lunch and the air conditioning in the plane. I realized I was not only moving to a different landscape, but also to a different mindset. Who in Israel would complain about air conditioning and lunch?

My cousin and I looked for each other for an hour at the airport and eventually found one another. I remember Ray giving her husband Sid driving instructions back to their home. "How come he does not know the way?" I remember asking. I knew they picked up relatives every week from the airport. "There are many ways to the airport in New York. Not one road like in Israel." A new life chapter was beginning.

My cousin lived in Riverdale, just outside New York. I stayed in her apartment and would commute to my classes at Martha Graham School everyday. But, in truth, what I really wanted was to find my own way.

I visited Rachel at her artistic apartment on 89th Street, and met her two wonderful boys, and began my American life by babysitting for them a lot. I remember the little one would not come out the first time and I had to win him over.

Through Rachel, I was introduced to Preston, whom I have already mentioned, a psychoanalyst, trained in religion and philosophy, who ran the Interior Life Seminar where weekly we read and discussed spiritual, philosophical and psychoanalytical works. We would study how these works affected and helped us to identify our strongest and highest values, so we could implement them in our lives.

At first, Rachel helped me since my English was rusty. Preston immediately understood my life. He said, "You took a risk." He meant moving to the States, starting a whole new life.

I told Preston about living with my cousin and not liking it. "Go and live on your own," he said. "You want to have a place to have your own feelings." And he was right. I had not crossed the ocean to once again become obliged to others and their expectations. I was writing to my parents at that point, writing every single day, guilt, guilt, guilt. I was taking classes in dance therapy, branching out, and I made a friend in class. Fortunately, she suggested I come live with her on East 6th Street as a transition, which I did, and eventually I found a place to live by myself.

But I needed a job. I kept applying for teaching jobs at Hebrew schools, but I wasn't getting hired. It felt like I couldn't break through the moat to get in. I told Preston and he said, "You will come across someone who will recognize your value and hire you. Just wait."

Preston also helped me to now take on the truth about my parents. He helped me to see them in their own context. The kibbutz was my parents' only home. Not only was it my mother's home who had no one of her own family left, but my father too was orphaned very young. His mother had died when he was 6 years old, and his father died when he was 13. He was brought up by older siblings and their wives. My parents both met each other in the Zionist movement in Poland, and had come to Israel to follow their dreams.

I began to understand how my mother had never got over her survivor's guilt. She never wanted to go back to Poland to visit. Whenever she went anywhere on a visit, she always wanted to return to the kibbutz. This was true even when we were in Italy living as a regular family. Preston said, "So when you expressed your pain to her as a child, she couldn't hear it. She might have been in too much pain herself."

And I knew this was true. When I was a child visiting my parents in the afternoon, I remember her lying down in bed a lot. She might have been depressed. In contrast, I was a child who excelled. My father was so proud of me, almost too proud. To this day, I am still a person who excels. I know that whatever I do, I must do passionately. But it was a responsibility, being the perfect performing child, the happy child, so as to cover for her, so as to cheer up my mother. I am not even sure my mother wanted me to entertain her, but I am sure I wanted to make her happy. So often I came to my mother with wonderful stories, to give her some light. I was brave, upbeat, hiding my own sadness, to tell her something to make her laugh. My father too looked to me to make up for all he had lost and to fulfill his early yearning. Many times on my visits from the States I had to ask my sister to join me to create a buffer between my parents' and their expectations. The blonde little girl with curls who continually strived to achieve. Now I find such focus frightening.

Preston wanted me to describe the kibbutz life to him in detail and Rachel wrote down what I said to make it clear. I asked Preston the most important question on my mind. How come I was the only one who felt the way I did about the kibbutz? Why did I feel I was alone in being afraid at night? What was wrong with me? Preston answered, "This is what is right with you. It is your sensitivity that saved you. You did not get support or consoling. That is why you felt so isolated."

Just we 24 children together all the time, with one woman, a metepelet and a teacher. So little adult supervision, so young and so many children. We must have had the need for a hug and a kiss? Consolation and tenderness were never available to us. We were free to victimize each other as children do. No one was watching.

When I met Rachel, it was the beginning of a long friendship that changed my life. Much later I made a comment that hurt her feelings and I felt heartbroken. "Don't forget, Sara, you are an answer to Rachel's prayer. She prayed to have a friend like you," Preston said. We were a beginning for each other. She wanted a friend to share her joys and sorrows. Someone to be close to her, as she had been to her mother in her later years. And in my case, through Rachel's love and support, I met Preston and started to look at my past and began healing and creating my new life for the first time. I never went to therapy in Israel which surprised me but, when I came to New York, I knew I had so many questions, so much hurt. Rachel was the guide that brought me to where I could finally find and expose my inner life. I was seeking to have a new beginning, I wanted to leave Israel behind. I must have known I had to understand it.

Preston's office had many books, and was on 5th Avenue at 95th. His office on the 3rd floor was utilitarian, male. He himself was 40, fit, slim, wore dark glasses, and was a real intellectual. My little one felt safe with him. He tried to understand her, was very open to hearing her. He saw us both as having a lot of courage, seeing him as a therapist and coming to his interior life seminars so fast. He felt she needed more therapy since there was a lot of rawness, a lot of tears, in her and me. I was lonely at the beginning in New York. "It takes ten years to feel home in New York," he said.

She had been through a hard time, he said, given how hard she worked on the kibbutz to try to fit in. When it came close to graduation from high school on the kibbutz, we were supposed to get a Medal of Maturity. You had to be worthy of this medal, and every classmate would come up for discussion in the group. This was a collective decision. It was voted of course that each and everyone was worthy. But one of my classmates went on and on about how self centered I was. What I cared about was me, me, me. I was curious as to what he was projecting onto me. Since I had leadership qualities, excelling in my undertakings and duties, I was voted to receive the medal but the discussion felt like a lynching. I knew that what they were discussing about me was that my nature indicated a certain independence. The fact I did not believe in my heart in the kibbutz philosophy seemed to show. That medal discussion was a preparation for how the kibbutz would betray me. Eventually this brotherhood would oust me.

Here is how it happened. After the first year of study in the school of movement and dancing in Tel Aviv, I asked the kibbutz to complete the second year of study. Decisions about kibbutz members were made in a weekly gathering, a large number of kibbutz members participating. At one of these meetings, they were discussing whether they should extend my second year of college, as they did for many of the young people.

"Since early childhood, she has shown signs she will never become a committed member of the kibbutz," said one teacher.

Another teacher announced to the assembly, "She is a failure of the kibbutz system, from early age." I could not believe it.

This was a great humiliation, to be called out like this. Many spoke of how I did not buckle under, even with doing well at whatever I was asked to do. They sensed that I was not willing to think collectively.

My father was at the meeting and asked the teachers, only what a kibbutz father might ask, "What did you do about those early signs?" Education was not in my parents' hands but in the teachers'. The members voted, and funding for my next year was rejected. This for a child of two very good soldiers of the kibbutz, this for a child who had been nothing but a model of discipline and duty. They were rejecting me for signs of independent thinking. It was a very devastating experience for my parents and they stopped believing in the fairness of the Kibbutz decisions. My family helped me return my tuition for the first year and I started life on my own. I began my 2nd year of school supporting myself, not feeling I could visit them because they were on the kibbutz which I now felt ostracized from, so when it was a weekend or holiday, I had no place to go.

My sister told me that others began to leave the kibbutz after my expulsion. Those who no longer wanted to follow the party line also left, some in the middle of the night. Things had changed. I had started a precedent. Apparently, there was gossip about my defection. Like those in Plato's cave, members began to ask," Is there really freedom out there?" I was called a traitor. My action let them know there might be another way of living. Years later, a teacher whose son was one of those who left in the night, said to me, "I am so happy you followed your intuition." Why did it take years for them to understand?

From then on, my mother refused to go to those meetings. And for a long time, I refused to visit the kibbutz.

Night

What I most remember is how nights were difficult for me. The yearning to be with my parents. I missed them so much in the Children's House, as I slept alone, with three other children in the room. Carlos used to always ask why I didn't speak of my childhood memories. It was because I had buried many of them as they seemed to represent a long period of acceding to a world I did not fit into. But now, as I write, I am remembering diverse acts of defiance, the spurts of my inner self expressing herself. Once in the Children's House when I was ten years old, I got dressed in the night and snuck out to my parents' home. Of course, they brought me right back. Recently, I saw a movie about another kibbutz and one of the mothers let her child sleep at her home and brought her back early the next morning. My parents were not the type to break rules. My father took my hand and walked me across the grounds and stayed with me till I fell asleep. I wanted to be with them. I believed in my heart they wanted the same. Something was very wrong. I felt it even then.

My mother once asked me when I complained about feeling alone, "But how can that be? They are there." She had no interest in what I was feeling. There was no validation for my real voice. How many nights I felt this way, impossible to count.

Even when I got older and was a young woman, again it was the night that came to haunt me.

I would have a coffee on Dissengoff Street each afternoon in Tel Aviv where I was studying, and then went back to my place all alone, left to a quiet Sabbath. All the loneliness landed on me on the weekend, Friday night. My friend, Nina, whom I shared an apartment with, went to her family. I was living in a 3 story walk up, and as I went upstairs, the sunlight began to disappear. When I entered the apartment, the walls got closer, and the silence would close in tighter and there was no way to escape or run away. She, the little one inside, was screaming at the top of her lungs. I fell asleep.

The next day there was more light around, so I headed to my aunt's and uncle for lunch through the sleepy, empty streets of Tel Aviv. On the way to their house, I heard piano notes bounce which echoed my feelings. The loneliness would pass the next day, Sunday, but those nights were long and empty, as they had been as a child.

There is a change in me since my marriage and since I started to write. I feel more on solid ground, so I decided to explore with some of my other classmates how they got through those nights. On my last visit to Israel, I met up with a friend who was one of the children who grew up on the kibbutz, Dr A and his wife Y. I was his leader in the youth movement and we always had a mutual respect. I wanted to find out if they felt the same about growing up in the kibbutz. It turned out he did not have any of the memories I had; he did not feel damaged by it. Maybe it is an issue of support. His mother was strong, determined, a dental assistant, and he has the same qualities. I venture to think he felt less helpless. I didn't feel someone was there. He was going to a class reunion when I met up with him and he was clear that he absolutely had no misgivings, believed in the kibbutz philosophy completely. He gave me the party line, but his wife, Y, had a different perspective. He came out totally unscathed, she explained, but she herself did have some conflict about the system.

This reality check confirmed for me that it was a mixed bag. Some felt the pain and others didn't. This talk made me realize my nights may have been hard because not only did I not feel supported by the system, but also by my own parents themselves. My little one had no one.

But I made a promise to my little one that I am not going to sacrifice her again. Now she will own her voice, so we can live a life where her voice is not shut down and is my guide. We have our mornings together where I listen to her at the coffeeshop. I felt this morning as I was walking my dog that she is digging in her heels about going to Montevideo tomorrow. She is not ready to start something new. My girl wants me to stay home, wants a routine, she is not looking for any changes. She is looking to be with me and to spend time together after so long being apart. I had been so busy up to now, repeating what my mother did with me, shoving her to the side and marching from one duty to the next.

Her longing for contact and connection is so intense and, as a young girl, was always thwarted. I remember I finished 6th grade and was going to high school. After school we were to go to work for 3 hours then back to our homework and each night a social activity. We were told that we would no longer have time to visit our parents. And she sobbed and cried non-stop. The thought of not visiting our parents was too much. Out came our metapelet who had got wind of my grief, and my parents came to talk to me. It was agreed I would have time to see them. Thus I learned that her little voice did and can affect necessary change when she speaks up or is listened to.

And because she spoke up, she brought about some magical moments in the night. Many times after the evening activities when I was a bit older, she and I did go to visit my parents who, fortunately for me, did not go to bed early. I remember the wonderful feeling of being able to show up at 10 pm and, oh joy, their lights were still on. What happiness that they were not in bed. We would sometimes have tea together in the teacups made of porcelain with delicate flowers reserved for special guests. It was not what we talked about that made it special, but it was that my little one was so happy to be with them and spend time together. It was borrowed time, unaccounted for anywhere in our schedule. A stolen moment to not be separated and to be a family.

Preston once said that the kibbutz separated my mother and me. Clearly the separation was a real blow to me, a lack I was always trying to fill.

It was a separation not only from my parents but my sister and brother too. We did go to our parents' house as children from 4.30 to 6.30. But, strangely, I have no memories of being with my sister or brother there. Where were they? My memory is blank. Did I need my parents so much I blotted my siblings out? I have no memory of playing with them there. When my brother came to visit me in New York recently and we had time, just the two of us, he was away from his family and I from my husband and it was precious time we'd never had. I had such joy making up for lost time, time never shared. Whoever came up with such a system? A system that was built on loss. Such an irony since the system was a response to so much loss of family in Europe. And then, they enforced loss on us in Israel.

A classmate recently reminded me that my parents were a home to her, since her father had died and her mother worked outside of the kibbutz. This too I have no memory of. I do remember talking with her on the day of her father's funeral when we were in first grade, memories are so selective, what stays and what is forgotten. Which is why I make a point of hearing my little one crying so she can get all her grief, all her memories, out. I don't want to force her to do anything against her will. She did that for so long.

It's so odd how the kibbutz came up with this strange theory of separating parents from children in the night when children are most vulnerable. Children are always imagining monsters and hearing things and they take comfort in their parents being nearby. But not at the kibbutz. When a mother came home from the hospital, right away she'd give her baby to the metapelet who was in charge and instructed the parents what to do. The theory was that she knew best, better than the parents how to bring up the children. That too much contact between children and their parents was not good, that if the children were sleeping over night at their parents' home, it would create sexual conflicts for them. In whom, I wonder, did they mean? Another theory was that it would be good for the children to be together 24 hours a day. But children don't need to be with other children for that long a time. They need quiet, loving care.

The kibbutz attitude to sexuality was confusing. They thought having children living with their parents would affect sexuality, but they seemed not to think, at that time, that there was anything odd about having boys and girls in the same room. Even as we got older, they boys and girls still slept in the same room, but I don't recall physical attractions. We even showered together, until we were maybe 12. We thought of each other as siblings. Our longings were for the elusive parents.

I can still, to this day, feel those achingly lonely nights. And then I thank God for my big husband, Carlos, and how he is my protection in the night.

In our bed
The warmth of his body
Are blessed rest.

I want more rest in my life. I love the feeling of being rested. We read in seminar a book called GOD SPEAKS (yes, I still go to seminar all these years later, it is a seminal part of my life) by a French poet, Charles Peguy. He writes about sleeping and resting and how not sleeping is not trusting God. In his poem, SLEEP, Peguy writes…"(People) look after their business very well during the day./But they haven't enough confidence in me to let me look after it during the night…./He who doesn't sleep is unfaithful to Hope. And it is the greatest infidelity… (They) can't be resigned to trust my wisdom for the space of one night."

In his long poem, NIGHT, Peguy writes: "Night…is where the child …accomplishes his being, Wherein he recovers his strength…. It is the days that emerge, but they have to be fixed in deep water, in deep night. Night, my most beautiful invention, it is you who calm, it is you who soothe, it is you who put to rest/The aching limbs/All disjointed by the day's work."

So true. For me, night was not a time of peace and renewal. It was a time of loneliness and anguish. And because of that, I have always wanted to extend the time prior to night starting. I remember the feeling of the world closing in beginning for me as my father with his light steps would walk me back at 6.30 to the Children's House. The lighter his steps grew, the heavier my heart became. The thought that I was going to find the hardboiled egg, our nightly dinner, no adornment, no help in trying to gobble it down, no salt, mustard, to be able to disguise the taste. And it was every single night. I kept looking for all sorts of solutions to the egg problem. Dropping it on the floor, stuffing it in the table, any way to have it disappear. Food was very predictable, no frills, no extras, no sweets, the same menu every week and the same hardboiled egg every night, not a meal to warm a child before she goes to bed. On Saturday we got an extra piece of butter for lunch which let us know it was Saturday.

After our dinner and the metapelet had already left, some of us would linger in the room where we changed into our pajamas and we would chat. This is a rare sweet memory of comraderie. We were the ones delaying the painful reality of going to the room with three other children who were sleeping already, delaying our staring and waiting and hoping to have the visit from the shomerat lila, the woman circulating between the children houses. Luckily, I was tired, and more times than not, fell asleep before she came. But I never got over my association of loneliness and the night.

I have no doubt I sleep best in Punta, with Carlos there. This is different from when I am in New York, and living in a non-doorman building, where I can get scared and feel unprotected.

When I cannot sleep in New York, I start doing something I did not do during the day. It is also daytime in Israel so I can make a phone call if I want to. Bust mostly, I practice my Spanish, or read. I know there is a coffeeshop nearby open 24 hours, and I can go there. I love that availability. I love that about New York. The city that never sleeps, the city that refuses Night. I think all these things and then I try to give into the tiredness, the surrender.

In the army the night was not as frightening. We were 25 girls in a bunker. We each had a gun but the real reason it was not as frightening or as lonely was they were not telling us not to feel.

And it seems that because I was hardly held in the night, I yearn to be psychologically held, even now. I like to see lights in the night, around the ocean in Punta, in the many buildings and it lifts my spirit. That light holds me. Light can be a beacon, a symbol of safety; and light is a symbol of spiritual awakening. When I went to teach in Sde Boker, I noticed on my first visit there were no lights on the horizon which immediately catalyzed the old feelings of isolation. Everything in me longs for an intimacy, not to be cut away, left alone in the dark. The dark in the kibbutz was especially frightening since there weren't any lights at all near the Children's Houses. There was something frightening about that deep darkness, especially for a child, and no one to run home to.

My father traveled a lot with his work, he was always coming and going, and this made me sad as well, knowing he was not there, not being able to imagine he could rescue me. I think now about his going back and forth to Europe and maybe he had his own soul darkness to carry. Maybe he felt guilty that he could not support or break my mother's sadness, maybe that was a darkness that he ran from.

This morning again I walked the dog in the misty solitude of the morning. And then to Boca Chica to write. My manager has not been so controlling lately, a little on the quiet side. Maybe he's changed his strategy. I am flowing with my book and he is letting me do it. I will have to start reviewing at a certain point. Writing makes me happy, it brings me closer to myself. I feel warm inside. My little one is more happy. She waited for this for a long time and this book is for her. I think I might call it The Sound of Her Voice. From years of being voiceless, her voice is being heard, respected. It is all about her. To let her speak. I denied it to her.

My dog is so happy to see me. I realize the connection between my dog and my little one. The dog is a manifestation of her, what she wants and feels. Unconditional love both ways.

I didn't make the connection before. He is her in real time, so open with his joys and sorrows. I realize how happy he gets, barking when I am on my way, and does not stop licking me. I let the dog sleep with me by my bed and it is her I am keeping with me all the time.

Coming here to the coffeeshop to write. Nothing is better. When I feel she is happy, I write faster. I keep my sunglasses on when I write to hear her voice better. It is the view inside I am focusing on.

The sunglasses darken the sun and I am returned to my subject of the night. It is where I was the most hurt because, I believe, it is at night that we let down our defenses. The manager is not at full form at night. My little one feels the most then.

I realize that many times when I go to bed, even with Carlos who is a home to me, as I close my eyes, I still feel the struggle with helplessness (no wonder the manager came into say, WE ARE NOT HELPLESS, WE ARE EFFICIENT), of knowing that, out there in the dark, there is no one who will come.

But of course it is no longer true. The dog comes and is always ready to make contact with me. And Carlos, with his warmth, is there if I reach out. There is someone there now. But sometimes, and this is the most damaging outcome for me from the kibbutz, she and I are afraid to reach out. We never learned how to and we were taught it is weak to want to reach out.

When I go away from home, the first night I wake up many times, the second night is better. Here in Punta, with the sea, and she safe here with Baba (Carlos) and me, I sleep the best. Perhaps as she speaks about it, we will get over it and let the dog and Carlos heal us, and let the light within and without fully touch us.

When You Feel Lonely,
Ask for More

At her little age, she did not have tools to deal with loneliness. But when I was older and began to see Preston, he said, "Here's what to do when feeling lonely, ask for more. Embrace it," and this became my mantra. A very good thing comes when facing loneliness. Years later, I learned to do as he said, to put it to good use and ask for more. In medicine, a bone that breaks and heals correctly is stronger than one that never breaks. That is what happened to me with loneliness. I feel the uneasiness and difficulty of it but now I let it heal itself. I stay with it. It is still a challenge, but I don't escape it. I transcend it.

In seminar, with Preston, we came across this Chilean nobel prize winning poet, Gabrielle Mistral. Her poems particularly resonated with me. She, like me, never had biological children. Her poems are about the baby she never gave birth to, about her imagined pregnancy, what she calls womanhood. All her poetry is a song to this unborn child.

"This child is as charming
As the sweetest winds that blow:

... His little body is so small
It seems a tiny seed so fine:
Weighing less than dreams weigh,
No one sees him, yet he's mine."

I think I dared not have my own biological children because my inner child had such a brutal journey, abused by the environment we grew up in. I would not be able to watch my child's helplessness and do nothing. I always admire people who have children, my sister and brother, a risk I could not take. I could come alone to the US, knowing no one, at 25 years old with only $500 but I could not witness helplessness.

Strangely, that was why it became important for me to make money. I did not want to feel helpless. I felt making money was creating opportunity, and it would give me options. I even feel I need options about food too. It is when I feel I have no choices, that I can have an anxiety attack. I will never be in a prison again. Enabling myself to have choices was a way to get rid of her inner screaming. I am aware I built a life in reaction to those feelings. The kibbutz was all about being for the kibbutz. I chose a life of self fulfillment.

I am reading a book where a girl has been abandoned by her mother and I see the pain of it. My little one felt abandoned by my mother not being able to mother, needing breathing space after the War and relying on the kibbutz. Her scars meant she could not mother on her own. My mother and I have that in common. I have such love and connection to children but was too afraid to have one of my own and, because of my little one needing so much attention, I could not do it. She is still licking her wounds, trying to grow up out of her loneliness into a shining light. We are doing it now step by step but, years ago in my child bearing years, with her endless crying in my ears, with having to wash her face from her tears, I could not come close to having another one to take care of. When I see mothers watching their children's grief without being able to stop the grief, without being able to help, I cringe. My heart is unable to live through it and endure it. I hear her voice and it overcomes me, with her little hands reaching out.

Recently when I visited my niece who just had a baby, a sweet one, and when I held her in my arms I was so fearful of her fragility and how not to hurt her. I was afraid she might break. Of course, it is my lack of experience but it is my little one as well holding onto me so strongly for dear life.

After I wrote today, Carlos and I went to see Buti, his son. We came back and it was a very foggy day. I went for my daily walk, striding fast and determined and, as I was walking, I fell. I did not see the wire in the street. A workman brought me home in his car. It was a minor accident but it sapped my energy, so I stayed in bed, talked on the phone with Paul, whom I work with, and my friend in Punta, Darrelene. I felt fragile all day, breakable inside. Is it connected to my exploring my feelings about mothering? I remember when Carlos and I were thinking about having children. We needed to take the next step of looking into treatments. But we didn't even talk about it. I knew. I had to get back to her, even though I was not communicating with her a lot. She would not let me have another child just like she doesn't want me to dance. She pulls me back and she holds onto me with such a grip to make sure I keep listening to her. She lets me know how I feel. I do want to take care of her. I do not have to agree with her. She was right. Having a child would have been too much and at her expense. Who knows? If I had a biological child, it might have healed her. That I will never know.

Any way there are so many children to love. My nieces and nephews. And I have 4 adopted girls, Elenora, Patricia, Serrana, and Bee and I was able to make a real difference in their lives. I don't think I feel regret even though I am very outside the culture of children and grandchildren in Israel. But through Carlos and his children I got to experience the joys and sorrows of having children and grandchildren. I used to joke I married him because of his children. I could not imagine life without them around.

> I thought I was courageous
> I travel long and far
> But not to hold my child.

Today she got up with a positive outlook. Not sure why but who needs to know? Again, I reread Gabrielle Mistral about her little one. What a pen name, Mistralis means the northern wind. This poet grew up in a small village in Chile only to become a Chilean ambassador. Another way we intersect, this love of South America and its being at the end of the world, in its beauty and humanity, even with the many terrible things that have happened here. But isn't that like life too?

My walk with my dog this morning was to a silent beach with no one around. I am thrilled with the aloneness of just the dog, me and the sky. In the quiet, I was reminded of how I was drowning in loneliness after I left the kibbutz. I wanted to be alone, but I did not know how to handle it.

Saturday nights in Tel Aviv signaled the coming week and hope. My boyfriend showed up sometimes. He was ambivalent about our relationship, since his family demanded he be with someone of "noble" breeding. They thought of themselves as high class Sephardic Jews from Iraq who took status very seriously, a reverse discimination. I was Ashkenazy from the kibbutz. I am not sure whom he ended up marrying. We had met in the Navy when we were both in Tel Aviv, after I finished my officer course. He was studying to become a lawyer, what else? A suitable profession for the "nobility." He was groomed for a lot. I wonder how his life turned out.

That was the most lonely time I can remember in my life, those weekends in Tel Aviv when I was going to school after the break from the kibbutz. It got better when I went to teach in the desert. I had a community and felt protected and held.

As I write this, I find the old memories are coming to the surface. In one of my recent visits to New York, I went with my old friend Kathy to Mostly Mozart, and we had a seat in the middle of the orchestra, 10 rows center. I always prefer an aisle seat, on planes too. The music was engaging, but I did not feel comfortable. I began to feel claustrophobic, with all these elderly people surrounding me and hardly able to get in or out of their seats. In the intermission, I got up and walked around and thought of staying in the back. I didn't want to return to the front and sit down in my seat. But I did and, then all of a sudden, I wanted to leave, I was --locked in. I had to get out of these rules, leave right in the middle of the concert. She could not stay there any longer, trapped. It had all come back.

As a friend said, "It is an alluring invitation to go to another level deeper."

There are so many ways to feel one's loneliness and embrace it, as Preston said. I was ten years old when my brother was born and he was brought home for the first time. It was very exciting. But it did not make me happy. I was confused and told to be happy. My mother was very preoccupied with him. I had so little of our parents and now this young new child comes (whom I now love passionately) but then… it meant more loneliness.

Elana, my sister, at that time also felt she was losing her mother. When my family returned from Italy, Elana was 6 months old. When Elana was older, my mother told her that she had been so happy to return to the kibbutz and give Elana to the Children's House. I wonder what kind of loneliness this statement is for Elana. But, at least, my mother shared this with her. They had a different relationship than I did with my mother, more chatty, more self revealing. I was the performer, held at some distance.

In a way, the kibbutz, by necessity, broke up families. The Children's House had to be the home. Your own brothers and sisters were not your family, the classmates were your siblings. It is an irrevocable wound to not have a family. That was why the weekends felt so alone in Tel Aviv. They took me back to not feeling connected to anyone. And even the weekends in New York when I have no plans for human contact will bring it all back.

"Did you feel alone?" Preston would ask me. "I felt so alone," and he asked, "Alone or lonely?" He questioned me when I kept on saying how alone I felt. He wanted me to really describe the loneliness. "Alone," he said, "is different. That is when you are being yourself as you really are. Loneliness is when no one knows who you are. "And yet Preston always said that haunting phrase, "When you are feeling lonely, ask for more loneliness. Do not try to escape it." A most unnatural request and yet the most difficult things are the most worthwhile, according to Rilke. Now I have the tools to understand these feelings and put them to positive outcomes. Apostocastasis.

He also quoted Whitehead, "Religion is what a person does in his or her solitariness." In my solitude, I try to acquire more and more skills. I keep trying to transcend my childhood experience.

Yesterday I was reading about Michelle Obama bringing Obama to her house for the first time and how taken he was by the size of her family, including all her cousins. He saw joy and what he saw he didn't know he was yearning for. He was longing to belong. We all have this yearning, for what could be.

For me, it was in New York and then in Punta that I had the chance to learn different ways, explore different sides of my emotions and interests and heal.

Preston used to say that he would take weekends and go to a hotel and grieve. Something I could do, I tell myself. I think about going to Montevideo, and staying overnight at a hotel, too. I have to work on my grief, it is spilling all over as I write and remember. Music is very helpful. I feel the need to find a place to facilitate this sadness.

The walks with my dog in the morning are the closest I come to it, but in a different way. They are of the true heart, like grief, but a breath of fresh air, just us, him and me, the sea, what a beautiful way to receive the day.

My Punta
Empty and hugged by water
Quiet sunsets.

I want to have the intention to be with her, I want to affirm it every day and be mindful of spending time with her. Where is she? Not quite sure. I lost some contact with her. I think for quite some time we have been apart. She did end up going to Israel with me when I visited, and loved it. We went to Eilon and she and I remembered the big trees. She enjoyed the walks with my sister in the early morning, coffee with my brother, taking in the breathtaking views of Galil and she felt somewhat free of the early nightmares.

She came back with me to New York and Punta. She was restless on the plane, where the service was unfriendly. She is very sensitive to unfriendliness, it brings her back to the cold inhuman treatment of her childhood. It makes her insecure. She starts to feel once again she has no one to turn to if she needs to. I felt she might go into an anxiety attack again. She takes over sometimes and loses control. I want to understand it better. I want to hear what is bothering her, write about it, for us to become more familiar with each other, to know each other.

After the anxiety attack in the concert, I wondered how to "manage" her. Is that how the manager was born? To handle her anxiety? I am curious but afraid of the feeling when she takes over and I don't know how to calm her down.

Preston said I have more anxiety than most people since "mother was not in the kitchen when I was exploring." Carlos gives me that. He is the wind beneath my wings. He gave me the backing I needed by just being there. When we sit on the terrace in Punta, we often remark how he helped me open the way to the future. He helped me, metaphorically, get off the street, to sell real estate and do it well.

Baba
He is there, regardless
Firm, steady, always.

As I get to know my little one, she is very demanding, has to get her own way. In fact, she scares me if she doesn't get her way. She is so interesting. As an example, the sky is getting grey and in comes a rainstorm and I realize that I forgot her. Turns out she was at the beach and I didn't run to rescue her. I was heartbroken at my leaving her like that. But she handled the situation very well, she realized it, she didn't lose herself, she collected all her toys, she came to the house and I bathed her, and fed her, and warmed her, and the dog came to help and be with her too and I felt so badly. I learn she is very practical and she knows how to take care of herself. I know that only too well. How much I love her, a guilty and passionate love, which I think is mothering.

I find she is also someone who likes solitude. Why the kibbutz was so hard for her. You can't have yourself without having solitude. As Mistral wrote, "Because in this stillness, in this quietude, I am knitting a body, a miraculous body with veins, and face, and eyes, and heart quite clean."

Solitude is not to be confused with social isolation or loneliness. Solitude is a state of mind where you can concentrate on yourself and your own interests, whereas loneliness is feeling some love is missing. In the kibbutz I felt isolated, there was no feedback. And I also felt I was the only one who had this feeling in the community, which increased my isolation. But solitude is the freedom to be contemplative, to be in dialogue with your feelings and higher thoughts.

My little manager, here he is, his agenda always breaking in. I am going to get a table for an upcoming fund-raising event, and even though I am here writing, he wants to start setting it up right away. She refuses to deal with him as they are very different and in competition. He is all business, powerful, pushy, and impatient. She is all feelings, spiritual, I think, yet she wants what she wants, too. She is willful, with no regard to time and place, impulsive somewhat. This morning she went with me to the beach with the dog. It was early and somewhat cold. She didn't care, she took her bathing suit, hat, and didn't stay long and then wanted to come with me to the coffeeshop which she loves. I created a little home away from home for her. They know us here and smile when we come in. They know what to order for us. She sits with me and plays under the table with her toys. Everyone notices her, she is so beautiful with blonde curls, not paying attention to anything, happy feeling at home, comfortable, welcome, having been met with a smile. She is finally not alone, she is with me. But let us not forget I am afraid of her temper tantrums, the child inside who is primitive, wild and demanding.

It is a beautiful day. The sun is coming up slowly and forcefully. In a few hours it will dominate the sky and engulf us with a strong feeling of spring. I am sitting outside on the street to take in the quiet moment. The dancing sea is in front and in back of me. It seems I am leaning towards staying here in Punta for a longer time. It makes me think how much I love the writing of Pablo Neruda. He had a love affair with the sea. He wrote…"Here I came to the very edge/where nothing at all needs saying,/everything is absorbed through weather and the sea/and the moon swam back,/its rays all silvered,/and time and again the darkness would be broken/ by the crash of a wave,/and every day on the balcony of the sea,/wings open, fire is born,/and everything is blue again like morning."

Isn't that what she and I are doing? Breaking the darkness and opening our wings?

"So, drawn on by my destiny," Neruda writes, "I cease-lessly must listen to and keep/the sea's lamenting in my con-sciousness…" The sea is deep inside me, too. Is it the love for the sea, or the power of the love one feels near it? It is 100% giving of yourself. It is so passionate, so enthralling, it leaves no room for anything else.

When one loves,
It spreads like the sea
Warm without borders.

I know my friend Ann, whom I met many years ago in the Interior Life seminar with Preston, will approve of my staying here in Punta more. We have become very close and supportive of each other's life journeys. It is an emotional connection because she recognizes her and and my writing; she has become a guardian.

I try to listen to my little one, but I am so afraid to let go and have her really speak out. What will happen? One of my fears is that I will go crazy if I really hear her anger and grief. Will I be able to function? Do I need to function? I might lose contact with reality, fall apart. Will I be able to put myself back together? If Preston thought I could grieve her losses when I came to New York, what is the problem? The problem is she frightens me in her intensity and vehemence. The word grieving is not scary, it is to let go that is scary. But Preston said I have a strong enough ego to go through it.

Gila tells me that writing is about letting go, letting whatever comes up come up, about embracing the past. It amazes me how out of touch I was with my fear of letting go. If one would have asked me, I would have said I have no fear. But the truth is I refused for years to come near the pain. The manager took care of it and still likes to. That is why he often tells me to stop this writing and let's put some plans in place.

Rachel, who is a writer, pressed me on my difficulty with writing. What do I not want to feel? Loneliness and separation from my parents? When I first came to the United States, I would babysit for Rachel's children to make a little money. She and her family helped me to heal the big hole I had about family life. I just didn't have the experience. I didn't know what families discuss at breakfast time. How do they get ready for the day? What are the routines of a family?

I soaked it in, their family life, and it was healing, embracing, a new world. Conversely, in my childhood, we were up at 6 am, exercising, and 8 in the classroom, 12 lunch and 1 to 3 working on the kibbutz, and then homework. But with Rachel and her family, I saw the continual momentary changing connections and, in their variation and love, I ended up rebuilding myself.

And then there was Carlos who healed my little one because he was in touch with her, even from the first moment. I was almost 28 when we met. We were at this friend's apartment on west 66th street, near where I lived then. Carlos was there. I was wearing a feminine dress, greens and blues with puffy sleeves, and later he told me he noticed that I had good legs. We started seeing each other, and he wanted it to get sexual but I resisted for some time. But Carlos stayed. I was teaching on the East Side and 82nd Street and he would pick me up and we would walk through the park. With Michael, my first husband, it was the opposite experience. He would pick me up in a car, and it felt like going back to prison because he was the choice of my manager, a Jewish therapist, forward moving. He turned out to be an empty suit, with no connection to my inner life.

But with Carlos, we walked through beauty, just being together. He knew quite a bit about art, and we went to the Frick collection, and he taught me about Corot, and other painters. In a very low key subtle way, we began our life calling together, me with real estate and him with his own interests and we were partners together. He saw her, the girl, and fell for the girl. And the girl wanted to be loved, be seen. She would only trust a relationship where she was part of it.

She has very specific ideas about relationships. She does not like those friends of mine who made certain judgements about Carlos which stunned her. She knows those remarks are not called for. She is allergic to gossip, having suffered the righteousnesss of the kibbutz philosophy that was against feeling, being. She and Carlos are masters of non-verbal communication, where trust grows. In The Little Prince, the wolf tames the little flower. How, the little flower asks, do I get tamed? We just come here every day, he says, and sit together quietly, consistently, and this builds trust.

She also loves my real estate business partner, Paul, because he is so much what he is, responsible, trustworthy. He never fails her, he is there when he says he will be there. He makes up for all the broken promises. She loves Elana, my sister, whom she didn't always understand but now we communicate beautifully. She is committed to my sister.

The wind is blowing softly and touching my pages reminding me of the softness in nature, the softness we missed as children, with the metapelet not having enough time for anything but our physical needs, food, showers. I don't ever remember her sitting down with us just to chat. When we ate together, we talked some. She told us about the book, *Little Women,* that she had just read. She had a happy spirit. She stayed with us for many years.

One time we called an all-out rebellion, turned the lights out and screamed and had fun before the metapelet was notified and came back to the Children's House to put a stop to the party. We were punished but it was worth it. Breaking the rules to keep free. It is good to come across fun memories buried among a lot of sadness.

My brother, David, and I, when he was in New York on a visit, talked about his becoming secretary of the kibbutz when it was being privatized. I saw his tremendous understanding of people, patience, wisdom. He educates me about anything I need to know about Israel. We are in constant touch and I consult with him on how to fire someone, how to handle people issues. I only tell him very little about this book, since his experience at the kibbutz was so different. Rules relaxed by the time he was born. It is my sister who asks me about it. She who is neat and has a fine love of flowers and beauty, who is vulnerable. She must have suffered there, and I am her voice too.

My mother, interestingly, wrote poetry. As do I. But she isolated, kept apart. Like Carlos, she carried physical weight. They both don't like to go out, they fight anxiety around it. And Carlos, too, has a beautiful voice like she did. She was a woman of standards, and values. As is Carlos.

Funny how themes compound in our lives.

My parents came once to visit me in New York. My father had been in the States a couple of times before. My mother had not. I was excited, and showed them Brooklyn as we were driving to New York, but they were tired. My mother shut down and it hurt me. She was not interested. This is loneliness.

One night I wanted to order Chinese food which my parents had never had. My father fought me, fought me, fought me but finally I prevailed. (I told you my little one is stubborn.) And then? He loved Chinese food! He could not get over it.

I so much wanted to please them, make them happy. My wedding to my first husband took place at the kibbutz, for them. A big celebration. Maybe I married him for them. Carlos I married for me.

My mother died 3 years before I married Carlos. She did not meet him. "Make sure he doesn't marry you for your money." Carlos loved (and still does) the essential me, the warrior. My mother was frightened of it, even though she respected it. Carlos is an individual, and what I loved was that he wanted me to be free of the sadness of my past, be who I really am.

Life is how you transcend your circumstances. It is about creating a second chance. I could never transform my life in the kibbutz, because there was no opportunity for it. There was no alone time to discover what my personal interests were, how my feelings created the texture of who I am, as all our feelings do. My life has been a protest against the loneliness of that childhood. And finding my own way and voice.

It is difficult to know how she is going to be and feel on a given morning. It is a rainy day and she wanted to run to the beach with the dog. But he doesn't like the rain. She loves him so much, but he hates the rain and we had to come back. But does the dog love her? He knows about her, knows she exists and is very comfortable with her energy. They are good friends. He sleeps right next to her. They hug and fall asleep together. He is like the teddy bear she never had, whom she rolls around with and laughs with when they play. Her curls jump up and down and she is full of joy and that is why I call her Sunshine. Her laughter is a belly laugh which is contagious. The people around her become joyful when she is happy. Why is she this happy when it is gloomy outside?

Golden curls and laughter.
Between joy and despair
Waiting.

Gas Explosion

There are many situations that inspire my little one to start speaking to me. The most unusual one that got her so vocal was when we had a gas explosion in our apartment in Punta.

Carlos could have died or been injured seriously but thank God that didn't happen. I don't want to write about it. It makes me so angry at Carlos for undertaking to fix the gas himself.

I was in the den with the dog when I heard it. Windows blowing out. A sliding glass door being blown onto the street. "Carlos?" There was a pause and I thought he was gone. I went into the living room. First I saw a newspaper had started a fire on the floor and I looked at Carlos and he was okay, one piece, standing up, but I didn't yet understand the overall damage. I went to get water to put the fire out. An hour later, a side window in the den fell, glass shattered all over. We were lucky and grateful that no one got hurt on the street.

At the same time, the doctor in an ambulance came up, checked Carlos' vital organs, and checked me. We were both alright, but Carlos needed dressing for his hand and arm. They were burned, raw and horrible looking. Why did he take this risk?

Carlos probably didn't listen to my warnings because he says when I repeat my requests, he shuts down.

I need to choose carefully when and what I say. I hate him today, after the blast, and scaring us, and it is okay to hate your husband. Rachel's mother told her at times you will hate your husband.

And then my little one became terribly upset, as if she was awakened from a bad dream. She was reminded how her skin felt when she was separated from her mother. Her skin felt like it was coming off, just as Carlos's skin did when the gas blew up. My mother too must have felt that rawness when she could not touch her baby.

Today feels like another brutal day. A client accepted a deal, went to contract, and now wants to renegotiate an impossible deal. Two years of work for nothing... worse than the explosion. The client, like all of us, wants what he wants. He is so convinced he is in the driver's seat. The anxiety of dealing with difficult people makes me want to run, very far so I can get it out of my system. I just walked and had lunch at a place that has a view of the ocean.

I pull my notebook out. I like being in Punta, even with all this. The waitress is pleasant and my little one feels safe here and life is not too complicated, which is saying something with explosions and deals that blow up. The seacoast relaxes us both, she likes me to be much less busy, just to be with her. This is what we never had, just to hang around together, being. Baba is good at that, being at ease and enjoying. No one is better.

I start to be grateful that all is intact and thank God for giving us another chance to continue our life, in our lovely apartment by the sea. However, the explosion and the deal still rattle me. Paul and I thought we would win the deal of the year award where you submit the most complex transaction ever, but one that works out. But this looks like it will not close, showing one never knows.

It took all the energy out of Paul and me, too. The client has a disregard for anything other than his money, he reneged. He doesn't understand there are other people involved and lives attached. All this fretting and anxiety is very typical of life in New York. All the waiting, screaming, yelling, getting us to lower the fee, pressuring us on an emotional level. I think it is a repeat of an old pattern of feed and starvation, dramas, highs and lows that I felt as a baby in the Children's House. I must have an attraction/addiction to the pressure of real estate, the highs and lows of connection. In some ways, I would like to just be me, free of this excitement.

Strangely enough, when I got back home the writing made a difference. I felt less anxiety, softened. The writing discharged my anger. I was happy to see that this work I am doing now is making a difference.

This is now the 4th day of our new life after the explosion. We are not taking our miracle for granted. Afraid to think what could have happened. Buti, Carlos's son, put it well, calling Carlos, "Ironman." He could have burned his face, or I could have burned my face. But we are okay.

My little one is inclined to be affected by everything bad that happens so she has chosen to ignore the details of this disaster. Beautiful and spirited as she is, she is fragile and changes on a dime. She is not steady, very much prone to ups and downs and I want her to grow stronger and have a tougher skin like I do in business. I get back up quickly. She falls into disappointments easily, I want to help her overcome it.

That night I dreamt of waves, me riding them and barely keeping my head over and being frightened of dying. I didn't drown with the waves, and I wouldn't let her out of my sight.

Maya Angelou did not speak for 5 years because she felt guilty for witnessing a murder that took place in the family. My

Sunshine lost her voice with the abrupt and brutal separations from her mother. My little one who was radiating life and joy, crumbled. As tiny as she was, she shrank to a size of a seed. She sobbed uncontrollably, she was wet with tears, cold and sad. Sometimes the metapelet picked her up, changed her wet diapers, but not her broken heart. All that she wanted was her mother, her smile, an embrace for her happy heart. My mother would come again after some time, more moments of bliss, of being loved, held, safe from my own bad feelings of rage, anger and fear.

Writing, I see, is its own road of discovery.

It is the World Cup in Uruguay and everyone is totally involved, noisy, emoting, rooting for their country. I write,

Their love for the game
Is in their DNA
May blue win today.

But how nice to be able to put aside all these noises around me. It is a decision not to hear. I think about her, instead. Did she learn to substitute her need for being cared for and held with games, distractions? How does one heal this deep wound? How can I stop from hearing her voice every time there is a separation? Will it ever stop?

I see the camaraderie among the people watching the games here. It makes me wonder when were we touched as children? After lunch, in grade school, we would go to the shower, to be washed by the metapellet, there were a lot of us to wash, and no time for any tenderness. We were in an army camp. I see that,

She's always crying
I cannot stop her voice
And wash her tears from my face.

Today is the first day, June 22, of winter in Punta, a sunny day, nonetheless. We took our solitary walk on the beach receiving the holiness of the new day. An invader has been there the last few times, an irish setter is walking on the other side of the street. Our private place is being occupied for a few minutes and then we have it to ourselves again. What a moment, us, the sea, the endless rhythm breathing in and out, quietly.

I want to be nicer to Carlos, come from a warm heart. His skin looks awful from the burn, but he is patient. He is working it out.

Woke up tired, perhaps the change of weather. I wanted to stay longer in bed but not the dog. Not sure if I want to keep him so close to my bed. He pushes me at night to be close, the way she wanted to be close to her mother, without any space, skin to skin to hear each other's heartbeat. I feel I can give him up. Maybe she does not need the contact with him. The writing may be helping her to feel strong enough to separate.

I am not sure what my walks to the beach and this book is teaching us. It is more like reflection, a short poustinia, a place to listen, so that she will no longer have her own life inside separate from me. That we become integrated.

Sometimes she is very social and loves to meet people, friends. In her happy little heart, there are stains that are slowly losing their dark color and becoming more and more light until the stains will disappear and grow in a clear skin. Not there yet but we are doing much better. I don't want to force her to grow up, God forbid, not hurry her, that would be another insult to her life. I want her to shine light through me so I can pass that light and love through to others. To be a warm supporting voice for those around me, less involved, more assuring without advice. I no longer want to rescue people (was that my way of rescuing her?) I want to be a guiding beacon, helping those I love find the right course and destination.

Like a lighthouse
She is spreading the love
To all corners.

I want to steady my spirit, no longer live between the bliss of our together moments shifting to a despair. No more of these swings I had as a child. I want to live in a spirit of joy, consistent and unshakeable.

A beacon
Against a full moon or storm
A steady stream of light.

My little organizer is so smart, he sneaks in every opportunity he can get to take over my attention. He's always been there but I don't ever see his face, it is not necessary. Moses never saw God's face but heard his voice.... But I am struck that my favorite prayer asks God not to hide his face. It is Psalm 27 and in it, "Hide not thy face from me; turn not thy servant away in anger; thou hast been my help; do not abandon me, forsake me not, O God my Savior." In my case, I may not see my manager's face, but he is always with me, he is my angel.

Listening again to Amy Winehouse in the coffeeshop, another survivor, however, who did not survive, and I feel connected to her struggle and get comfort from her singing. When I came to New York, and I moved to live with Judy on East 6th Street, I used to listen to Billie Holiday and she gave me courage to get up out of bed and put one foot in front of the other. Billie did that with all the struggle she had to go through, she got up and sang.

Listening to my little one also fills my heart with love since listening itself is transformative. When listening, I completely disappear into just listening which consoles, heals and makes me feel more love for her, my dog, Carlos, and my friends.

My conscience is clear regarding the deal. I did what I needed to do. We did our work and provided our services. The seller was not honoring us and our work, by asking us to reduce our commission, he was wrong. So glad we stood our ground. Maybe I feel good because of a sense of justice. How could he take our work for granted? Not so uncommon in real estate.

But I have a part in this, too. I was too afraid to lose the deal, the exclusive, and I had not spoken to him from strength and I allowed him to take advantage. He was giving me a hard time about being in Punta, objected to my being here. In the end, it has nothing to do with what we are doing. At the end of the day, he had taxes to pay, and he thought it should come from our commission. We did a great job for him and all he talks is the bottom line. It is a shame how much time and energy it is taking from us. I hope emotionally to be able to learn from this, to feel liberated, and feel detachment.

My body is slowly waking up, carrying the pains and burdens of yesterday. At my age I can't ignore it. My dog and she are on a different timetable. He is ready way before my aching body is. He sits, jumps and plays in expectation of our walk, our special time of the day together. I put on my scarf, gloves, get a leash and here we go. At least she and I catch up to him. There is no wind, the palm trees are motionless, no waves, no foam, only the sun hesitating to come up. We are here to witness this fleeting encounter of the moon with the sun and this vision imprints our heart.

> It is only him and me
> Greeting the holy moment
> When new day meets the sea.

As I write this morning, I am happy I did not go too much into my heartaches of yesterday. A break from temporal time. Writing is the authentic relationship for me, so unlike when I hid what I felt among 24 children, out of fear of their cruelty to my vulnerability. I went underground with my feeling. Now here I have the consolation of the written word.

Punta gives me what I missed as a child, a holding environment where I can stay even with the ups and downs of impinging reality on my life. The quiet uneventfulness of life really resides in the in-between, as Winnicott defines the holding environment, a calm flow. The mothering of Punta's sunsets and sunrises. Punta gave me this till my house caught fire. But we are getting back to serenity.

And yet I also realize there was a black hole in my heart all my life. This brutal early separation left its mark, taking me into periods when I kept returning to those huge black holes. I see her reaching out without any response and, each time, my strong heart which accumulated many years of experience got a crack in it. My heart was strong, hers was hurting.

> Stretched out arms.
> Another crack in my heart
> Waiting for me.

Praying Carlos' burns will heal soon without infection. Carlos' exterior wounds keep manifesting my interior ones. I suppose to see such vulnerability kicks up my own. My Carlitos with his raw skin, all torn, peeling off. He is in real pain, bedrest will help him to recover.

> I barely walk at the beach
> The sea is breathing in and out
> And the warm sun.

She was too young to know that her mother would return to her. She had no idea of time. All she knew was the moment together, happy, fed, held, united, warm, then in a dark hole alone.

I felt I was on fire with hurt and longing. It was an open burn without any salve. The pain only stopped when my mother or the metapelet picked me up.

Of course, as she grew older, she began to realize the mother would come back. The beginning of healing. She could soothe herself. She now had knowledge. She began to know the pattern of when her mother would return. She grew and was able to understand and hope. In Spanish, to wait and to hope is the same word. All my life I worked to heal, to be free of the conflict with my young environment. My little one was with me the whole journey, step by step, but I still did not take the time to just be with her. But she waited for me patiently. She is the one who had to learn to wait, first between feedings and then she waited so long for me to find the courage to go back to her. She waited much better than I did. It pains me how long it took but I knew I could not die with out going back to her voicelessness and skinlessness and listen to her.

She got up in a good mood today maybe because Baba is feeling better and his hands are covered. She and I took a shabat walk which made her happy. I hope I can drag her to the dance class. She dances when the music comes on, but when I go dancing, she doesn't want to dance, she sits on the side and pulls me down. Maybe my being free without her frightens her. Walking she loves. She is an active little girl jumping up and down. She has control of my spirit. It is so hard for me to be happy if she is sad. I have to converse with her in order for us to continue. When the dog is by my bed, he is so soft and loving and I feel this warm energy coming through me. And he is always there to receive it. He feels the love and basks in it. She takes part in this ocean of love, too, where the spirit and the body totally unite with the energy of love. There are no boundaries when the body and soul are one.

It is May 1 in Punta and I am in Boca Chica, where I write. The singer sings to heaven with a voice full of yearning which touches my soul, bringing me to tears. It is a holiday today and almost every store is closed. It brings me back to closed doors, no options, when hope is shut off. I always need to make sure the door can open. This is part of my fascination with New York. Nothing is closed to you. Today I eat a medialuna croissant, something she wants. Maybe being in touch with her voice makes me be good to myself. I realize this morning how much it takes out of me to go back to my old feelings. I need to put the fire out in such a way where I can transform the feeling of the fire into understanding, where I realize these are just memories. Part of my expectation of the writing is that it will diffuse some of the urgency of my feeling, and make me recognize them as they are, memories.

I booked my tickets to return to New York and I will fly Copa, a Panamian airline. Carlos says this kind of neurosis of the German pilot who flew his passengers into death could not happen with a South American pilot. The German pilot who kept his door closed as the other pilot banged, begging and tried to hatchet the door open. Such helplessness, despair and his not listening. As when my first husband just got into his car each weekend and left, no matter how I felt. When friends in New York don't make time to see me. A closed door. Annihilation.

Punta has light. My home has large windows to see the sunrises and sunsets. Light has possibility, openness, the opposite of closed doors. Preston always told me, "You need a lot of freedom." That's because I had no freedom on the kibbutz. Everything was regimented, proscribed: when to see the parents, how long, the belief system was even prescribed. There was not too much freedom intellectually, spiritually. The doors were shut.

Soon I will be leaving for the airport, and the upcoming separation from Carlos and the dog feels raw and sensitive. The tears are right there, a door closing, if only temporarily. Recently, when I was in New York, I felt so much pain at the separation after a phone call with Carlos whom I couldn't reach and touch. It was so intense that I thought I will take the first plane and go back, but I also knew it was a flashback to her and how she felt time and time again.

It is only here in this city hugged by the sea with loads of light and almost an eternal Spring that I can step into the place I need to go. I am held enough here to take a deep breath and rescue her, the love of my life. I realize as I take note that my leaving her behind was what my mother did with her family, left them all in the painful, burning house in Poland, to never see them again, her father, mother and sister and little niece whom I never knew she had.

It is funny that I never know what will come in writing. That is why I think I will always take time to write. Why is my manager all over me today? In general, there is nothing specific to take care of and he is so busy. I understand it when we have to take care of things. Is it the trip to New York looming large? He never rests, he does not need or want to rest. He keeps me up unnecessarily, afraid he is not keeping his eye on the ball and that something bad will happen to us. He is vigilant, hard working and very worried always. It is his way to keep us going at all times but he does not know when to stop. He gets up, makes lists all the time, what to pack, what to buy, who to meet, and when I sit down to write, he dictates the tasks of the day. He is very controlling, everything he does with a sense of duty, very responsible, never leaves anything to chance. It is not easy to live with him. Does he ever relax, enjoy life? I wonder how he feels about me bringing her up.

He does slow down in the evening, early too bed. He is not too sure about Carlos, but he knows not to push him. He knows Carlos takes his time. They have a mutual respect. Maybe my manager has his own family outside of us that he goes to after he finishes. He is with us a lot, maybe he had one that he lost that he does not want to talk about. Which means, once again, that my manager is tied into my mother and the family she lost. She and my manager are very matter of fact, both of them would never get into feelings. It is funny that I think my manager is a male when really he is a part of my mother, her not wanting any feelings to get out of control.

I know there was good in the kibbutz system my mother so loved. The philosophy was that we were our brother's keeper, that if we could, we should do what we could to alleviate the difficulties of other people. It was our responsibility and this value was born in all of us in the kibbutz. We never had a sense on the kibbutz we were missing out on the rewards that capitalism was offering. We were equalized. We wore the same clothes, we ate the same food, we all had the same opportunities.

So many conflicting thoughts about the kibbutz. I recently saw a movie about another kibbutz and the film interviewed people about how they felt about the system. One woman said, "I felt like a queen, princess, when they took the baby away." One person's child was taken to the hospital and the metapelet did not feel the need to tell the mother. One mother said, "I am a woman who loves to hug and kiss and I wanted to be with my child but I was told it would excite a sexual feeling and I had to stop doing it. Stupid me, I believed it."

Didn't they know that a mother, even the worst mother, is better than a metapelet? A mother has an instinctual knowledge of her baby's needs and she adapts to them (Winnicott), giving a feeling of security. Now some of these children of the people they had interviewed have grown and they do not have a relationship with their parents. They cannot get close, there is anger. The grown child's attitude is they weren't with us when we were afraid, so why should we go be with them now? I had felt that too. Some were not even close when they were children. I myself couldn't skip a day of seeing my parents but there were children who didn't even visit their parents. They had no interest.

What we had, and were supposed to be held by, was the righteousness of the kibbutz philosophy. We had a sense of pride in our devising an equal society, one for all. The kibbutz felt that men should be equal to women, that this equality eliminated sexual harassment, but this of course was not true. Of course, there was sexual tension.

In the movie, one boy's father died and nobody asked him how he felt. No one came to console him. He went to someone else's father's funeral and burst into tears. There he let himself feel, and the class looked upon him as if he was a freak.

In other words, with all this physical closeness, there was a tremendous lack of deep emotional caring. We never talked about how we felt, even though we were together all the time. We did our tasks, school, work and nothing for fun. When I began teaching in New York, the kids said it was not fun. I was shocked. Fun? What are you talking about? My experience had been that everything was duty, a military goal. No time for leisure. I did not make one friend. I was friendly but nothing like the friendships I have now.

My brother and sister, on the other hand, had life long friends in the kibbutz. But much as I love my sister and brother, there is no doubt they are guarded in terms of feeling. We didn't exchange our deepest thoughts. It changed as we grew up, intimacy has grown, especially with my sister. They are very good people but the heart was meant to be secondary to duty.

When I was in my last year of high school, I did make my first true friend but she was in a different kibbutz. We had gathered from various different kibbutzim in Kivatviva. We used to interact with people from the same movement but other kibbutzim. Nina was not born on the kibbutz, she was a Russian Jew who came to her kibbutz much later. Already it was evident that I wanted something different. She had a cousin in the kibbutz that she ended up in. She is exquisitely beautiful, and came with her twin brother. They were like orphans, and looked upon as second class citizens for coming from the diaspora, not in the kibbutz elite. There was a superiority complex in being Sabra, born in Israel. She was mistreated as all children who were not born on the kibbutz were, and did not return to her kibbutz after the army. She is still in Israel, married someone from her kibbutz, has 3 children and grandchildren. She started painting very recently.

Nina and I were roomates when we both studied physical education and dancing for two years in Tel Aviv. We were witness to each other's life. She and I had a tremendous affinity, although we were very different in ways. We recently got together in Tel Aviv and it was as if we never stopped seeing each other. We stayed in each others' lives and continue to support each other. She is as beautiful as she always was. As before, we share our critical lens of life on the kibbutz.

I am writing and I am glad it is in English because, if I ever publish, it will give me some distance from my classmates who will be up in arms about it. It is funny but writing is easier for me if I eat. It calms down some of the feelings that come up. Rachel says she eats nuts and they keep her company.

To give the kibbutz more of its due, it gave us a tremendous work ethic and discipline which I like. We were taught the philosophy that where there is dirt, why don't you take the broom and sweep it? Don't wait for other people to do things, you do it, and get it done.

People thought the kibbutz would take care of them forever, be the good mother, but it was not true for everyone. When they privatized, it became apparent the first generation were left without any pensions, like my father, and had to fend for themselves. The second generation of my brother had to shoulder the responsibility for many of these older people. The dream of everything forever being taken care of had come to an end. That was a gas explosion for many: and it can be a gas explosion for many of us. To have to grow up and fend for ourselves.

Friday Nights

There is a Jewish poem that says it is a sin to be sad on a Friday but I am. Carlos' skin burning is hard for me at the moment, seeing his pain, and then my memories. But the sight of the sunset helps.

> It is Friday
> Sadness is descending and engulfing me
> An all white garment.

But I know enough to know that I need to steady my spirit. I had a day to myself, bought lunch in the green market, squash soup, and went for a massage. Carlos had gone to Montevideo and was having a difficult day with one thing and another going wrong. But I worked hard not to react, to stay in my life. Elenora and I lit the shabat candles, I got my hair done, walked back when the sun was almost down, a few remnants of dim light in the far distance where the sun touched the sea. The night was approaching. Walking along the waves on the boardwalk by myself, I was ready to receive the shabat. Because it is now winter here and many people are away, there was no light in the windows of my apartment house and no one in the building. But inside, I felt a feeling of expectation, anticipation, to receive the shabat. I lit the candles in my own home and said the blessing and that perfumed the air, and then I made myself a shabat meal. Salmon, baked potato, broccoli, and the lighting of the candles and blessing of the wine added a sense of holiness to the moment. It was a moment in my poustinia, a little desert, and one can create it at any moment of the day, a certain experience with yourself and solitude, just being. I held onto the spirit of this Friday evening and did not get busy being worried and preoccupied with Baba's hardship. He called late and I was in my shabat mood and he was relaxed and on his way back home. He asked that I not ask any questions about the day. He did not know what I was feeling, that I felt much less curious, less involved. He did not know I am growing wings and that I am not hovering over him and not in the middle of things anymore with her growing up. We are changing and trying to be an angel-like spirit, helpful but distant. Later Carlos arrived, tired from a long long day, and we did not need to review the events of the day. We could talk about anything that needed to be discussed later. I fed my hungry dog and I was assisting Carlos with the activities round the house. It was a nice day, the triumph of the shabat spirit continuing.

She used to love Fridays. I still do… I used to ask my metapelet, Is it Friday? Do we have a kabbalat shabat? WIll we light candles?

Is it Friday, she asks
Looking for the special light
To celebrate.

She had this spark. Friday brought joy to her little heart. But it is curious, looking back, that we new Jews never prayed, holidays were not religious. The goal was to be fulfilled by the social life on the kibbutz, not religion. Not to say there were not some wonderful facets that did have spiritual implications. We had a very extensive music education, including all instruments, choir practice with a music teacher from the States, all of which gave us a tremendous love for music. Nature was such a strong part of our lives and nature is spiritual. To this day, I have a powerful affinity with sunsets and walks in nature, particularly in Punta, an island surrounded by the sea, and in Galil where I grew up, an ever-changing landscape where gentle mountains meet the sea.

When I left the kibbutz, Fridays became my most lonely time. But when I moved to Sde Boker, a college of the desert, after my schooling, it was there that I learned Fridays were special. I was part of a group of people who gathered every Friday, had a meal and had very inspiring conversation. I was not lonely there when we got together and shared the beginning of shabat, I felt protected and a part of the community, maybe like the kibbutz but one in which I felt I belonged. Now I light the candles every Friday. I love their light and the blessing of shabat. But it is loaded. It is the time that things shut down, a day of rest, of holiness, my best and most difficult moments happen then.

In New York, when I arrived, I used to fear the empty open weekends and was always looking to make plans to be together with friends. Now, when I am in New York I am so busy taking care of things all week long that being home alone is not so difficult. Still, I value so much the concept of a special day to go inside yourself. I love this poem about the shabat:

> if we forget to rest
> we will work too hard

and forget our more tender mercies
forget those we love
forget our children
and our natural wonders.

I don't think you can celebrate shabat without a home. It evokes the most sweetest of memories when I can let the light in, and take the time to have a visit with the spirit.

I find integrating with her brings me to a more detached place, more spiritual, much more steady, much less affected by daily life and that is spirituality too, not to be too affected by the ups and downs. I feel more whole in my self. To be consistent in joy, a stream of light, unshakeable. Listening, rather than feeling I need to give advice. My organizer seems to be on sabbatical. He is letting me just be. We are all learning to just be.

A sunny perfect day
She stopped running all around
Shabat is on its way.

Home

Even before I get to New York, I am busy on the phone fixing up my home in New York, making it just to my liking. My new home, which is a redoing of my apartment in my Charles Streeet house, is for my inner poet whom I think is her. I remember when I went alone to visit the poet Pablo Neruda's house in Chile. I was unused to taking a trip like this by myself. I booked a tour to his house which did not materialize so I got a driver to take me to Neruda's ocean-side Islanegra house, which was full of of atifacts from the sea. I had lunch and visited the house and something about it was thrilling. First, I was surprised because I enjoyed making the trip alone. Ann, my friend, said, "You sound so great when by yourself." Which is not natural to me, but my inner self resonated with the trip deeply. And then there was the whole idea of his home. This is where his writing and he thrived. This book is a home too.

In fact, home can come in many forms. Shul in New York feels like home and where I chose to have my 70th birthday party. New York itself feels like a home. Carlos of course is and was my first home. Punta, with its quiet and beauty, is now a home. Seminar is a home for me after all these years, with our community of shared values. And flowers, flowers are always a home and they make a home.

It is the end of the World Cup and so Punta will be quieter. Germany won and Carlos said, "There is no substitute for winning." I am writing in my coffeeshop, Boca Chica, and Carlos asked me to join him on a trip to see his son, Buti, which I agreed to. We could not reach him, though, so I was left to write. My writing is becoming a way of life, especially getting right to it in the morning with a fresh head and not postponing.

My home in New York will be my beautiful refuge, a Zen palace, minimalistic, white walls, full of art, a smaller kitchen, the whole place like a whisper. The window treatments will allow the light to stream in. But what is going on with me? What is this writing about? My new home? As she grows up, I am changing the environment too. Making my home a reflection of the new me, clearer, cleaner and everything inside. It will reflect my interior change. The thought of the change really excites me. I will have beautiful dishes, towels, art, and I know it has to do with the writing as well. I want to have a beautiful place, like all the beautiful places I find for my clients, not be a shoemaker who has no shoes.

St Theresa says the body is the temple of the soul. I think the house is the temple of the body and the soul. Even here in Punta, I hang my huge picture of the sunset. I feel inside a change in me, she is happy, jumping up and down that I am decorating our apartments here and there.

Last night Carlos was not in a good mood, and gave me a lecture about a raincoat. The good thing is I didn't react. I once took a course on communication and it said to leave the argument on the floor, don't engage it, it is not yours, leave it on the floor for the other person to look at his own issues.

Carlos feels I am not home with him enough. Today I am not in the best spirits, but I am trying to stay in the lighthouse, on an even keel. It is difficult when I speak to my niece, and hear about the ground forces in Gaza. She shared with me how she lost her baby and I was happy she felt close enough to tell me and now she has to process it emotionally and take time.

Today is a perfect day. We walked to the beach, just the dog and me, such a treat. I listened to the tape Elenora sent me about what she is studying. Finally, I heard it to completion at night when I could not sleep. It says that illness is when one is in the wrong environment. One needs to be aware of the stress, remove the stress, change the environment, and become aware of what causes the stress. Stress is the cause of illness, her tape says. They took samples of a gene cell and divided it up into four different environments and the gene developed in four different ways.

I went to the coffeeshop to write and, as I was walking here to write, I felt I did not want to come here to start digging again; it is hard to write every day. Renovating my place in New York is what I want and need. I have to finish with sign offs, plumbing, design, there is much to do. I never gave it to myself before. I thought a lot about it but did not have the money, the time, or felt I had the right to do it.

Last night I woke up upset about when I had sublet my apartment, and they had left it in such a mess. The feeling of violation kept me up. This whole thing with my house and writing has opened up this entire subject of home. I remember when Carlos visited me in New York before we were married and he said I had been able to create a pretty place to live, but he felt no one was living there. It was perfect in that everything was in place, but it felt lifeless to him. That was then.

Her home is her temple
A sacred beautiful place
To be.

The townhouse renovation is a real gift to myself. Preston said that every time he came to my apartment, there was a change, something new. I am a person who changes.

I sell homes so that I can witness the moment when a family or person sees a place they can call their own. A sacred moment, an emotional encounter, and it is an honor to be a part of it. It is a vicarious reparation for me.

There are all kinds of vicarious reparations when you do something in another set of circumstances. When I help an elderly person cross the street, I imagine I am helping my father. In my case, I heal something in myself by seeing other people and their excitement about their newfound homes. It healed my own need. That's why I went into the commodity of real estate rather than stocks, bonds, futures etc. My little room in the Children's House was a place to sleep, not even to rest. It was not a home.

When I returned from the army, I got my own place in the kibbutz. I always treated it with much love and attention. It was a studio apartment, and I remember washing the floors on Friday afternoon, waiting for my boyfriend to visit. After I finished college and I was teaching in the desert, I had my own place in a row of apartments there. When I moved to New York, I stayed at my aunt Ray's home, a godsend since I had just arrived in New York, but it came with an obligation as well. I became the companion to my aunt when my uncle was sick and dying and I extended my stay there in gratitude for a while, defying the reason I came to New York, which was to find my own way.

After a short stay with my friend on East 6th Street, I rented an apartment from a friend on west 93rd and Central Park for the summer. It was lovely, a place one could call home. I had a record player, and I bought a few records of classical music and felt in heaven. I had a taste of home and being on my own. I remember the surge of feeling of such happiness when I played Bach's cantatas, a feeling I had never had before, being in my place with music.

I then got a lovely place on west 75th with a terrace and then moved with my first husband, Michael, to Lincoln Towers, 2 bedrooms, 2 baths. After we split up, I got a studio in the same building on the 20th floor, flooded with sunlight in the morning. The building went co-op. I needed less than 2,000 dollars for a down payment. My friends gave me that money to buy the studio. Carlos moved in with me later and a neighbor bought our studio and we bought a one-bedroom, coming up in the world. Then we bought this wonderful house in the West Village, with trepidation, but it was the best real estate decision I ever made. We renovated it and, after Carlos decided to move back to Uruguay, we ended up renting the upper duplex and we moved to the parlor floor. That home was able to afford me the life I lead.

Preston always said you have to have your own place to have your own feelings. A home does not come naturally to me.

A place to be
To think to feel to cry
To know I have survived.

Missiles from Gaza are flying close to the airport and they have closed the airports down. I want to go for Rosh Hashanah, and stay in a hotel. I see I am writing bookkeeping issues, some way of taking a break and not being focused on her and her feelings. Yet Israel, at one time, was my home too.

Got up in good spirits. Carlos feels better, hope he sees a doctor before I leave. I am learning how to deal with him, to suggest things, to keep the morning quiet. He is very slow, and allergic to me making plans – my manager.

My little one loves when I talk about home, she loves when we are staying in a hotel. I work so hard, I should give us this.

My home
Years of yearning
Home sweet home.

Today my pencil barely writes. My organizer is working full time, knowing we are soon going to his city, New York. I am grateful for having him on my team. She is feeling better knowing that I will ensure us safe homes both in New York and when we travel. Home is a place to feel secure. I love that I have the one in New York which is mine. The one in Punta is Carlos' and mine together.

Back from Montevideo. This morning Baba went for early tests. When he returned with the dog, he seemed happy. He has lost some weight and we were all happy and went back to bed. Somehow I managed to annoy him by saying something that he interpreted as controlling. I see his point. I should have said nothing. It was not an attempt to control him. "Why do you have to always have the last word?" he asked. It is not a matter of the last word, it is a matter of explaining. One reason I married Carlos is that he stands up to the organizer in me. It was she who married him, not the organizer.

It is easy to get Carlos angry. A match ready to light at any minute. My little one goes to pieces. She wanted to leave the house and have lunch outside. She told me how happy she is going back to New York soon. She feels, in order to stay married to him, I need to take those breaks. I also need to develop a thicker skin for his anger. She really understands that to handle his fits of anger is not to engage with them.

Funny how it all started with a happy moment, the sun is out, and then! she is full of hurt and rage with his comments. I read it takes 90 minutes for those types of feelings to pass. To sit with them, and then they will subside. Anger is a way to manipulate. It's a false power, shuts people down.

We are forever young, vulnerable, it seems. Our temper together was huge. He is afraid of words. She feels he is not a fair fighter and she is right. He has something with words, shuts them off. I am glad that I am going back soon to New York. But the truth is that the anger passed away and the rage was gone. I could breathe easier and so could she. Flashes of anger are part of an inner and outer home, too.

Open the door
A wind blows in
Creating chaos.

In point of fact, she has a temper, too. When our house got violated by tenants in New York she got furious. She stormed in having a fit, stayed up at night and questioned me time and time again: Why did I let other people stay in our place? I tried to explain to her I thought it would be good to have more money, she didn't feel this way at all, we have enough money and so much more important to keep the place for us, and the family too. I find this dialogue interesting. I am listening to her and her fury. It is non-negotiable so I made my decision the house is only for us.

It is great when she shows up like that. It is about her, this voice. I had to really calm her down with the house. She was sobbing and we talked about our time together in the

Children's House. Don't you remember how lonely we were? How night upon night we waited together for the shomer lila to come by so we would be just a touch less afraid? To be comforted? For someone to touch us in bed, to assure us all is okay, and the next day is coming. How many times we waited. We cannot even count. How did we survive? She kept on challenging me. I have a lovely place and to open it again for strangers who come and go and do not honor how hard it was to get there? What about the tears and the sweat to have a place I can call home? To love is to surround yourself with books, art and music and all the comfort that was missing, and I gave it away. We shared for too long. We used up all our sharing time. In subletting the apartment, I repeated what was done to us. It's a habit and it was taught me as a philosophy… it would be selfish not to share. But I have the right, and this is the first time I am discussing it with her. She is still angry, I feel it and maybe we need to be back there together and then she will feel better. I can't wait to be there with her.

Our home was invaded
Carelessness
Opens old wounds.

Israel

Israel is under siege. Elana is driving to her daughters to help out. She lives alone, so it worries me. I take comfort that Elana has a close neightbour and she could turn to her. Again, it is about being close. I live so far away and this is the cost of our separation.

> She is not afraid.
> Alone in the street in the car
> The missiles are falling.

The news from Israel continues to be scary. Underground tunnels are what Israel is dealing with, and these tunnels are terrifying. Bombers wait in the tunnel and blow themselves up. It seemed one soldier was kidnapped. It is so frightening how many are willing to die in the name of Allah. How many lives we lost clearing the tunnels. The cost is huge. The idea of why they dug the tunnels and so many of them in order to cross over to Israel and attack is a travesty. How could we let this happen? She is so scared, so worried, I cannot find her this morning.

I fear for Israel's existence. Many times, I have thought I should find a place for the family to escape to and I was thinking of Barcelona. Carlos said to take time to think about it, but it was the first time he joined me in seeing how difficult it all is and my trying to find solutions.

Most people see what is happening in Israel and identify with the underdog. Hamas wants to kill as many Jews as possible. The anti-Israel sentiment refuses to see that, and I include Carlos and his family among them. (Even the UN is anti-Israel.) They don't understand that I feel this whole debacle about safety on a personal level. Not politically. In New York I am a member of a community in a shul, there is shared experience and an understood deep care for Israel. In South America, I am without a sense of such a community.

But we Israelis are perceived as strong and the world identifies with the weak and helpless, the Palestinians. Peace has to come, we have to work on it. Going it alone resolutely is a big part of the Israeli identity and I feel I became financially independent partially as a defense. I, like my country, felt too vulnerable about the possibility of being caught in a situation and not having my needs met. After all, that is what my little body experienced in the kibbutz.

And we were not as strong as we like to think. Even in the kibbutz, we had classmates with serious psychological issues. One of my classmates was fondled against her will and left scarred. One had a tendency to steal. Two of my classmates committed suicide. None of it was addressed. It was all left unattended, no feeling, good or bad. It was all about survival. The country is founded on wounds, and we are supposed to rise above them, pay no attention to them. Yes, the IDF is incredible; it feels it has to be or the country will be annihilated, but we are not a race of Tarzans oppressing other people, as the world often likes to think.

Busy night with Poppy, licking himself. I kick him out of bed and he cried and made a scene. Carlos got angry with the noise.

Since I was awake, I went back to the news. There were bombings of schools and hospitals in Gaza.

Carlos also got up. He repeated to me: 85 women, 135 children hurt, a lot. Terrible.

I tried to explain that the Palestinians are using the women and children as a human shield. I understand his identification with them, but it is my people, my country, my family I worry about.

She used to be, I notice, very afraid of Carlos' annoyance, but now we are no longer afraid. Wow, she is going through her own process, and different now that she is vocal, being taken care of by me. Things are not how they used to be. She is very respectful, but she is not backing off about what she believes in. She is a strong girl, and feeling more her strengths, creative energy, which is manifesting itself in many ways. She is willing to have less control, and is not ranting and raving but going right to the heart of the issue.

It is interesting to realize this book is even changing my marriage! New parts of me are being expressed. Her previous voicelessness manifested into a need for affection that is now changing, with her giving me (and Baba!) arguments. She's growing into expressing her feelings.

Carlos then admitted that he too is worried about what is going on and came to me and apologized. He hopes it does not affect our relationship, these serious disagreements about Israel. What can I do, I wonder. Support Israel and make my family happy and there we are.

I can't find her today. She is upset with me, maybe about being so preoccupied with Israel and not her. Maybe she needs a break to digest our experiences. I see her as she is in my photo, in a blue dress with white and red stitches (the dress I gave to the community). She has many curls and a big smile. So sweet and generating light. I have to look for her and find her.

I should write for 45 minutes without looking at my watch. That way you are growing a muscle, because writing takes a lot of energy, mining yourself, finding the words, re-experiencing the feelings.

Yesterday I stayed home, resting… not sleeping. I had gone so early to the beach in the misty morning and came back to rest the whole day. To just do nothing. Still not in the best of spirits, feel very isolated after admitting to myself about South America's non-support for Israel. Darrelene, who lives here, at least responded to some information I sent her. She was able to admit that Hamas is playing a part and a big one. We Israelis have to have a leader from the left who will bring a new point of view to this whole horrible situation. I am going to start praying for it. Even, with all that is going on, I write:

Unimaginable
Warmth and glare of the sun
Soothing the soul.

So many people are envious of and hateful about Obama. There is too much hate in the world, hate only leads to destruction. The situation in Israel is looking endless. Bomb after bomb. How long will it continue? I was surprised when I reached out to my friend in Israel and saw her Facebook post. "Netanyahu should choose to do the right action without any criticism from the US." I was taken aback by her comment. Israel is not independent of the world, we have to act accordingly as a neighbor and as part of the rest of the world. Such arrogance on the part of Israel. Rachel pointed out that a lot of education is needed. The intensity of my friend's feeling and disregard for the Arabs surprised me.

My little one is around but she is not too involved politically. She lets me handle it, it is not her concern. I think her concerns are around survival. It must be she who got so frightened about the tunnels. A real fear of extinction. The Palestinians get in and kill so many soldiers and this surprises and makes her feel anything bad can happen. I try to calm her down and give her information. Information always helps. To get in touch with the hate toward Israel is frightening for her.

The other issue with her is my weight. She is so afraid of being hungry, starved as she was between feedings and one egg every dinner growing up in the Children's House. I thought I could approach eating less quickly and then she will not feel hungry. I need to work with her so I can have a body that is mine, not one that I keep from holding onto past deprivations and holding onto my mother.

It feels good when I am writing from her voice. The good news is I am writing every day. Her feelings have also improved my haiku.

But I go back to feeling anxious all too easily. I am so disappointed that Israel is leaning more and more toward revenge and conquering by force. What a wrong direction. Maybe the left will find a more pragmatic approach, not something that makes people feel good in the short run. So hard to watch TV, enough is enough. I watch Charlie Rose and they made a very good argument on the Palestinian side. When it is quiet, the Israelis keep with growing the settlements. I pray for a miracle of some kind, someone stepping in new, and leading Israel toward peace.

There is something in the Jewish psyche that feels isolated and recreates it in the world again and again. There is anti Semitism all over the world, no one is on our side as we wish yet we go and attack our only friend, in this case, the United States. Netanyahu is preoccupied with Iran and is doing nothing about Palestinians. Maybe that is his strategy and God only knows there are no shortage of threats to Israel. He is focused on that instead of dealing with the issues at hand which is Palestinians.

Rachel also is very sensitive to the news in Israel. How could we not be? This is our homeland where we grew up, where our parents crossed borders and sacrificed everything to build this beautiful country of ours. I am so happy my parents are not around to experience this round of hostility. As Preston said, with each war, moral values deteriorate.

Dark time and alone
With the crushing waves
Standing.

This morning has too much going on and not enough time. I hate to rush, it crushes my spirit. Rushing is horrible for one's soul. Got back to reading Amos Oz and cannot get over his talent and ability to describe a situation. Master of all masters. Glad to be reading him and find we are addressing different issues in the kibbutz life.

Try to get back to the few books that are by my bedside. Desert Fathers by Thomas Merton, Rilke on Love and Other Difficulties. Letters to a Young Poet did not grab me this time. It is interesting how certain readings can be so timely and coming back to them is not the same.

I don't feel her around so much. She is busy with other children. She is more relaxed, more on her own, more independent. I love it. She looks great, happier than ever before, many more smiles. Not sure what she wants from me. To just stay by her side and be there when she needs my help, I think. I can't believe how much she grew in a very short time from a ball of sorrow, from being untouchable, to having a nice new skin, pink, and fresh. Still thin but growing and growing strong. Like the skin on Carlos' hand which is almost back to himself but not quite.

Today I am not pushing what to write about. I feel Carlos is more at peace with me leaving, not happy about it, but not depressed, resigned in a good way. Not sure how she feels about the trip back to New York. She loves Carlos and Poppy very much. It is hard for her to leave Baba. She loves the simple life, she loves nature. New York is too busy for her. But that is where we are going next.

My girl
Before saying goodbye
At the beach.
Leaving
The spaces between us expanding
Showers of tears.

New York

We are at Rosemary's, the coffeeshop I like to write in when I am in New York. It is at the corner of Greenwich and Tenth, open and full of light like Boca Chica. There is beautiful classical music playing, high ceilings. It is quiet, and here I am, back home trying to return to myself. The house was in good shape but every time I look deeper, I find things I don't like. Drawers in disorder but, all in all, the house is clean and the flowers in the boxes outside, cascading and colorful. I have a list of things to do this morning, the most important is the renovation which cannot wait. Still not my home sweet home but it is mine and I love it. Can't wait to see many movies, another option for me to get in touch with feelings. Today the manager is working diligently… this is his town.

Yesterday when seeing Paul, my real estate partner, who is Polish, hardworking and kind, I felt it is good to be in real estate. I am shifting the lighthouse position to shedding light and warmth around the business regardless of what situation we are in. I feel grateful for the privileged life I have. I love when Paul sends me an email, "No worries." When he was selling his apartment, there were many bumps in the road, and he was very calm and, in general, that is the way he is. I love him and I very much love this quality of his, among others.

Today is day two in New York. I am in the French Roast on Sixth Avenue but still in the West Village, sitting outside on the sidewalk, my spirit feeling the need to roam free, with unplanned activities. I might come back here. Something is crowding my spirit, not sure what it is. Yesterday I did not write and was not sure why not but, today, the outdoors feels nurturing. I am wondering if it is the shift and such a busy calendar which takes the air out of me. I did not bring my phone with me and now they start digging in the street. No shortage of noise in this city.

Breakfast
Omelet, tea and blasting noise
My New York City.

It is encouraging to see that, after writing and eating, I feel better. These mornings are short outings and this might be the place for me to work in New York.

After I had the Open House with Paul, I went to the Village to the Michael Kors store and bought a ring and then went home and crashed, feeling depressed. I am not reading. I felt hungry again. That is what I am craving and feeling: to be satisfied. Yet too much food scares me, big portions depress me. The evenings are dangerous for me, it is left over from the Children s House, the loneliness of the night there. It is still with me at 70. Will it ever go away but I recognize the feeling, like Milerepa's monkeys. Can I make friends with them? Being hungry is damaging since it brings up memories and most of them unconscious. I want to be very careful with my monkeys: Hunger, night, and loneliness.

I need to be free. Not be controlled, to be able to come and go, not report to anyone, to live a life completely unlike my childhood. I saw the movie The Room. The mother and child lived in such a tiny space but there was freedom there. They were confined but they had themselves. Something that was not allowed in the kibbutz. Even though the boy in the story had a distorted sense of the world, which we did too by the way, he and his mother exchanged their feelings about it and they shared their love. They were able to examine life in their talking, and the kibbutz, conversely, had closed down any discussion of our experiences. The kibbutz was like the room, in that food was supplied, we were stuck there, and we had no idea of what the outside looked like. We thought we were better than the people on the outside, but it was not true, there were good people living in the city too. In the film, there was no brainwashing, and real truth was exchanged.

Being outside, in the air, in the noise of New York City, at French Roast, something feels free. Still on somewhat shaky ground, not sure what causes it. Does it have to do with my writing? I keep opening old wounds, looking deeply into them. But I feel I am good company to Rachel, Paul, Kathy, when I see them, which is reassuring that I am not crazy and gives me the feeling I should embrace those monkeys, those parts of myself that sit on my back and weigh me down. I loved so much when Mark Bergash in seminar said to embrace them and befriend them. My grief is up to my eyeballs, I have to let it out and find ways to release it. Rachel is so good at this, a real example, she has the gift of tears. I should learn from her and really start to facilitate it. For the first time I shared my writing with her. I respect her opinion, and took my time about showing her, and she used the word "astonishing." The whole concept of my little one surprised her. I am trying to explain she is separate and yet part of the whole person. Rachel wanted to know if she was me or not me? I never really analyzed it and I don't think I need to. I know her, and my book is about her. Maybe it is another personality in me but who cares? It is me and part of me. She has a life of her own. I love her and I need to be in touch with her.

Rachel and I went to a seminar on a five-word memoir. I wrote, "She is voiceless no more." It tells the story.

Barbara Corcoran in one of her talks gave advice on how to handle the morning: Do the most difficult thing first. That has been my method, too. When I get up, I start with the most difficult phone call and it gives me self respect. She also talks about visualization. The other suggestion is Steve Job's edict to live as if it was your last day. If it was mine, I would want to see my best friends, Rachel, and Ann, meet with Gila who is all about writing and we understand each other, and then I would have a salsa lesson. Paul would be part of my last day too and of course Carlos. No mention of my family. I have been living far away from them all my life. Work I can take or leave on my last day. I would love to be in seminar on my last day and exchange ideas on the spiritual life. Thank you God for the love in my life and may I be able to spread it, Amen.

Today when I got up, I tried to visualize my day. I get such strange pleasure sitting in the middle of the street in the middle of the noise, the chaos. In New York it is summer here and I am sitting outside like I do in Punta when it is summer.

There is not much difference between my last day and today. I pretty much live the life I want. I make good use of the changes that take place in Punta, my going there more often, which was at first a challenge but now it is in fact the best place to write. How strangely it came into my life and then my townhouse that affords me to not have to worry about making a living.

It is Friday
The hustle and bustle of New York
I miss them (Baba, Poppy and her.)

I had wanted to write in the quiet of the city, and so, this Sunday, the empty streets feel beautiful, some Punta in New York. I certainly will try not to exceed 3 months away from New York although the transitions take a toll on me.

I met with Gila today about my writing. It was life affirming how I am going about the writing and the relationship with my little one. I felt so good with my work. I raised with Gila my lack of description, and she said not to be worried about it, that she has a raw voice trying to be expressed, coming out of her and that is the story. A certain feeling of freedom here in the French Roast, movement inside and out, people rushing.

After a talk with a friend, I realize that I don't like to always talk about my little one because she is fragile and hidden and she doesn't want to be narrowed down, defined by explanations. I am not even sure she came to New York with me. She did not join me at the airport. She is really scared in the city, but now I see that she did show up at my place. She does not go out like I do. What she likes best is connection with me and it is not about New York for her.

Sometimes I could be talking about Carlos. She seems to have the same feelings as Carlos. I told Gila that when I am not in touch with her, I don't feel I am writing.

I know she came because she does like some parts of New York. She likes the walks by the Hudson River, she likes to stay in my little bedroom when she's very close to me. She likes small spaces. The warmth. The fireplace and the art, and she likes being in the apartment alone when she has the place to herself. She likes the little bedroom with the light coming in, and is still not sure if the owl outside my windowsill is real, even after he moves his head around. She watches the pigeons coming closer. She is shy, very very shy. But there she is below my bed, she loves all the blankets and pillows inside. She feels protected.

She also loves the Jewish community in New York, it provides her with a feeling of security and safety, and she roams around the synagogue doing what she wishes. She, similar to me, likes the noise of New York, it gives her privacy. In New York the noise pushes you into yourself and you are forced to listen.

Ann is one person with whom I love talking about her. Ann seems to adore hearing everything about her. How is she? Ann asks. Ann is attached to her vulnerability.

Sunshine never developed barriers. Is she going to grow up and leave after the book or will she stay around? I don't think we will separate. We are together.

Since I now feel she is with me, I begin to get attached to writing. Sitting in my corner of Elephant and Castle, another quiet restaurant in the Village, I am enjoying reading this book about the Morgenthaus. In the memoir, which I enjoy so much, I admire Lucinda's love for her husband and his love for her. At times she crosses the line with her rebelliousness and neediness but she is always concerned about him. What a pillar he is in his community and family. Men can go through so much, having to handle the outside world. He had five children and the early loss of his first wife made it a challenge to hold his family together. Everything about their love touches me deeply. How they broke up before the wedding (I also got scared after my wedding ceremony, as I stood on the Argentinian hotel steps. I feared the lack of freedom.) I wonder if Morgenthau's children read the book. I hope not for their sake, because in some ways they were very distant from her at first, and she speaks of the pain in that for her. They were not so welcoming to her, keeping quite separate for awhile. I had a very strong connection to Lucinda, the writer of the book. I saw myself in her.

After Lucinda and Bob got married, life changed. Marriage and living together are very different. I had the same experience. What changes is the commitment. It is reassuring, as deep as one can go. You are now family.

Started to write with so many distractions, and then took a quick visit to Susan to her Jefferson Library garden which is an oasis in the middle of the city, a place of peace, with its flowers and trees next to an ornate Victorian library. In the summers, they have musical concerts in the garden.

I notice with my clients how it gives them liberty of spirit when I let them have their feelings. When I let them decide if they want to work with me or not, and when I am detached. I tend to be able to read their emotions. This came from the kibbutz, I am sure. Children are masters of intuiting through nonverbal communication. I had watched everything as a child since no one would listen to our voices. And now I use that skill in my work. I can see who is selling and who is buying. Even when the client says they are buying, I know it might be a year or two later.

It was the same when I came to New York and was applying for jobs to teach movement and dance. I went here and there, and everyone said I had no experience with American children. Preston said, "Sara, someone will see your value and give you a break."

After many interviews, I interviewed at the Mamaroneck Day School, a Yeshiva in a spectactular setting in Westchester.

After a brief meeting, I met with the principal and he told me right away, "You got the job." When that principal moved to Manhattan to teach in Ramaz, a yeshiva on the Upper East Side, he wanted to bring me with him. I had to interview again with the principal there and got the same questions again, "What is your experience with American children of this age?" I had worked with younger children and these children were in high school. And I said, "I don't have that specific experience. "He said, "We need people who know the rules of the game." I said, "You are absolutely right, you are a prestigious school, you deserve the best. You should not hire anyone less than that." He ended up hiring me on the phone because of what I had said. I gave him liberty of spirit which makes people free to choose. God gives people liberty of spirit, even to refuse salvation, according to Preston.

If I could have my dream, I would be a philanthropist, as Carnegie was, Warren Buffett now. I do it by donations to causes I care about, and by helping people, like I do with my cleaning woman, now that her husband doesn't have a job. I help people, in little ways that make a difference. I long to give of myself in small, quiet, discrete ways.

Not in the best of spirits today. I begin to miss writing (did not do it for a few days, very difficult when the manager starts working here. He is so busy.). What to do first, how to write, today is somewhat a wasted day. Made plans with Kat, wanted to see a streaming of an opera outdoors. We missed each other at the Whitney Museum, and therefore we had to give up our plan, instead of what we wanted to do. The good thing is I saw friends, walked and maybe will do some shopping. I am so occupied here. For some strange reason the noise helps me, it makes me feel in motion, it is a kind of music. Today feels about me not her.

I need to get the frustrations of business out. Putting them to paper makes me feel better, am beginning to get used to it. Once I get them out without any judgement, without any other opinion, I can move ahead.

The visit to shul was divine, so hard to get there in the mornings. Writing comes first, this should be a habit. But Rachel was definite about going to shul, and I decided to go there too. I took a cab. Few people were there. I felt like I was home again, being there with my people. Kiddush. When the last war broke out, I went to the shul in Uruguay and it was winter and not open. I needed to be with my people and there were't any. Here in New York, when I went to see my doctor, he and I spoke about Israel and at the second appointment the second doctor spoke of Israel as well. New York is very Jewish and that feels like home, too. I should seek out the Jewish community more in Punta but it is hard. The Uruguayan president said, Israel is committing a genocide. This is how they see Israelis there.

Writing is not a priority in New York, so much going on. I realize I have an aversion to crowdedness. I truly hate it. There is so much around here in New York. Droves of people. So glad I had a quiet night at home, no telephone calls, only Carlos who was not feeling happy. I have too much human contact here. I slept pretty well last night, looking forward to less pressure. I so much want time here without many responsibilities, just going along quietly. My manager is all over me this morning, he's competitive about organizing. He is very definite, never takes into consideration how I feel, just how I perform.

He is steady and strong
Keeps me in line at all times
Down or up, by my side.

As the day goes on, I have a disappointment. But it doesn't pay to worry, does not change the situation. I have to wait it out. School has started and families are around taking their children to school in the Village.

Transitions are hard, such as going in and out of New York which is difficult for me, or even going from work to home. It is good to notice this and work around it. Preston talked about that hour when coming home after work, and quoted a poem for me which I can't locate. Watching the sunset is a transitional time, too. Apparently, in mental institutions sunset is when patients go crazy, when day turns into night, brings a certain loneliness. The hardest time for newly separated couples is also this time of day. No one is coming home to make the transition with them.

New York is all about privacy and, with privacy, comes loneliness. New York is the most lonely city, Preston used to say. I was so surprised when Ann said she does not feel lonely. I feel it every day. I feel it coming home from the office or from activities outside. The loneliness of dusk as the sun sets. Yet I love sunrise and sunsets, Preston said, "That is because everyone can enjoy them. They are available for everyone." In New York, we rarely see the sunset.

Noise all around
Digging, traffic, kids back to school.
But her voice.

I sometimes drop her, not even give a thought to what she is doing or where she is. Does she feel abandoned? New York can drown out the interior life. Bells ringing add to the cacophony of noise in the street. The mundane and the sublime. A new day.

There is no question that my writing suffers in New York, and I feel bereft of losing it as my friend. As I sit in the coffeshop, a woman (with a dog) is helping to put a sweater on her mother. I wish I could have had the chance to do that with my own mother. Between reading how Lucinda Morgenthau felt about her father and the kindness in her mother-daughter relationship, I get tears in my eyes. My grief is spilling over, but I am still not crying enough. This stalled grief stuck inside me causes me many times to get up on the wrong side of the bed, or to be overweight. The intensity of my writing focus has slowed down. Part of me is afraid to go to Punta and part of me wishes for it and the real ability to concentrate on writing there. Very grateful for the mobility I have. I just said hello to a fellow broker passing by and it is wonderful to be part of a community as well.

Mother and daughter
She gently helps her out
Putting on a sweater.

Funny how we each are our own personality in a family. My sister has my father's love for home and cooking and a life more centered in one place. Carlos is like that too except he is more philosophical, like my mother. I am all about freedom, my soul wants to see.

But New York also takes away some freedom by keeping me so busy. And I see that, in order to channel my grief, I need to be alone to attend to the inside and let go of visits and activities. Hope after this visit to make better use of my time in Punta. It is amazing that, even in Punta, I have to be mindful of my time. Life is so open ended there, but so full at the same time. I want to move inward with much less socializing. Socializing does very little for me. At 70, you really get on board with priorities.

Punta Del Este

We are back in Punta and I am second fiddle with Carlos. It is
she who is with him. He is good to her, kind and soft, loving
with her. Yesterday we dropped Carlos off and I came back with
the dog, ate an empanada, and the dog cried non-stop till Carlos
came back home. I feed him, I walk him, I am fun. But they
are alone together a lot, and the dog walked around the house
moping. My little one feels exactly the same way about Carlos.

After I met Carlos the first time, he took me to his office,
and he showed me a picture of his children that was on his
desk. As long as I live, I will never forget how he looked. His
heart jumped out of his chest into the picture. Bebe, his son,
sent a picture of our new granddaughter. We are crazy with
excitement. I just wait to watch how Carlos looks at the photo,
the smile that comes over his face. He gets right into it, and
I wait to hear what he has to say. It is his connection to love
that I admire. What words he will use. Our daughter-in-law,
Paula, says it is such a joy to get up in the morning and find
this little toy in your bed.

I listen to Mozart's concerto for harp and flute which
makes me cry. Sometimes the grief takes over. It's like a cloud
and when tiny parts of it clear, it makes my day better. I think
I had a good day yesterday because of it. After 70 years of

holding back my tears, letting it out is a challenge. Without doing that, I cannot move forward.

It's funny how I hardly ever go out at night here, as I do all the time in New York. Sometimes Darrelene and I go watch the sunset, but I don't go out to dinner, since people eat very late here. I love how different it is since it gives me the opportunity to explore other sides of myself. In New York, one always has too much to do. Writing is number one here and I have to make more time to be with Carlos. I sleep so much better at night here because Carlos is around.

The sea
Stretches his waves across
Smell of watermelon.

It seems getting back into life here is easier. I walked the dog in the morning, a breath of fresh air. It is quiet, and the quiet lets me hear my soul's desires.

My Punta
Empty and surrounded
Water, quiet, no waves.

I am beginning to like parts of my book. Had fun making up a story for Carlos about the dog, how he ran off and what the dog thinks about. Beyond pleasure. My little one, the writer, is secure and happy here. I noticed it as she told Carlos a story, playing with him, about the dog, and Carlos noticed my new freedom in creating like that.

I had to present at seminar, and I was nervous, how to organize it, the 12 Steps of Humility, but when I sat down, my notes came together. I made the material my own. It had a shape. How humility bring us to the truth, which others feel too. The seminar lifts my spirit. The seminar is living in eternal time. It is one of my homes.

When Carlos and I sat on the terrace and read the headlines in the paper about successful couples, I saw that one of the many things he did for me was help me to open the way to the future. I became more successful after we were married. I was able to focus, feeling supported.

Baba
He is there,
Regardless.

Sitting outside in Boca Chica, no one else is sitting here. Want privacy and quiet to get back to my work today. Reading May Sarton's Journal of a Solitude is great companionship. She loves and writes poetry, and said she would write even if no one read it. I share her love of flowers and nature, and resonate with how she describes the sunlight shining on her home and flowers. She has a fascination with light and how it enables her to encounter herself.

She says she can't have herself without having solitude. The reason may be that solitude is a deliberate choice. Solitude is not isolation. Isolation is more a state of mind, where you don't feel connected to life.

It's October in Punta and the sun is coming up slowly and forcefully and soon will engulf us with spring heat. I am sitting outside on the street to receive the morning, the sea in back and front of me. I feel relatively still inside and out. It seems I am leaning toward staying here for longer periods. My little one beams as I write this. I am her guardian. It is beautiful to guard what is precious in each one of us.

I just walked to Boca Chica. But, even here, it is hard to leave the house, to make the time and space to write. A beautiful day and I already walked my dog, came home, cleared off odds and ends and made a coffee. Seminar took a lot from me but I enjoy it. It is an investment of time. Seminar work always renders me results inside. And I loved the challenge of putting myself into the hard work 100% wholeheartedly, with 100% concentration. Santayana's reading was challenging.

Carlos and I doing better, he lives in a different world, and sometimes we argue. The question is are we better off after a fight, I am not sure. Do we have a better understanding of each other? I think the answer is no. Fights are usually power struggles, exhausting emotionally and useless. In Path of the Just, Luzzato talks about not being hurt or offended. Free of insults, not retaliating, it is something I want to do better. Not to begin the fights with Carlos. It was because he criticized me, ignoring all that I do positively for he and his family. I very much want words of appreciation. He generates warmth but he does not articulate his love, he demonstrates it. My desire for acknowledgement reflects my inner wound of not getting my fair share as a child. There was no time for that in the kibbutz, no individual attention or individual feedback. I react so strongly when not appreciated.

And that is how I remembered Punchy. Punchy is a new character for me. But one who has always been inside me. He is physically small and stocky, wearing red all the time and he is ready to punch and jump the gun. In the beginning, he was busy reacting to my hurt nonstop, ready to argue at any minute, ready to get into it. But with time and in the process of healing, he is punching and reacting much less. He still is ready for action at times and he always gets me into trouble. But lately, and with my writing, he is much calmer.

Punchy, I realize, works for the manager but he can be vigilant and act on his own. It amuses me to be in touch with him. I can see he likes being acknowledged. Even so, he gets most into action with Carlos.

Spoke to Rachel about my struggle with Carlos and how important it is to feel compassion. Jesus needed to come down and identify with the people first so they would trust in his compassion (St. Bernard). He made the effort to understand the language of humans. Preston said the greatest compliment you can give a person is to make an effort to speak their language, to try and see what they are seeing, not see just through your own lens. Well, I do feel compassion for Carlos. I get angry because I get hurt.

Rachel asks, How? I want Carlos to think about making me happier, having a coffee outside the house, celebrating my birthday, buying me a gift. He did help me to celebrate Passover, maybe when I ask him something specific, he will comply. Maybe I just need to be clearer and say what it is I need.

I went out last night socializing. How little it does for me. There is conversation but I don't always find that people relate. I don't want to gossip, exchange judgments. I wish to stop doing it since these judgments come from the same mouth that talks to God. These types of conversations are in contrast to the purity of seminar. Rilke stayed away and was careful of social life. He believed it can be toxic to writing.

Didn't get up in a great mood. Walked to the beach with the dog who is beyond beautiful. Maybe it's the grief pressing in. Rachel says it is not such a big deal to write and let the unconscious' stream of thoughts come up. I am not sure. My organizer (my mother?) is constantly on top of me making judgments about my work. I am being critiqued. I feel an outer eye watching over me the whole time. My writing coach brings a gentle eye and it allows me to reveal my writing. Precision, tempered with gentleness, is a powerful combination. Today I am afraid to meet myself with the writing. That may be because I am still unsettled by socializing. It's the subject matter on my mind right now, real connection versus false connection. I want to be very careful and do what nourishes me, my family, my writing. Social life can detract and it did. I disrespected myself. I got caught up in this wind and I want to be careful the next time. I will have to thank this bad social experience for the teaching.

Great walk by the sea alone with my dog on the beach. I just love it and he does too. He is so demanding, "Time for our walk," he nudges me. When we come back, I am supposed to cook for him, he eats and then goes to Carlos. His routine, not even a question.

Carlos, I notice, is so different than the manager. He is afraid to plan in advance. He does not anticipate, and does not see things coming, but has an attitude that we will deal with problems or obstacles as they happen. "En el camino se arregla la carga," he says, which means "We arrange things as we go along." There are pluses to his approach. I am the opposite. Half way to Carlos' son, Buti's, I am worried about a fight the dogs are going to have and, he is right, they may indeed not have one. My fear is my anticipation.

My approach has helped me in business because you have to anticipate otherwise you fall flat on your face and find yourself surprised. It is good to anticipate in business so you negotiate with more options.

But, in reality, I need to live every day in rythym, have plans, but live in the moment. Move from my head to my heart more and maybe with less of a schedule. It is good to have some guidelines, but I think rythym has to do with lack of rigidity and listening. I need to look inward to put on paper what is going on inside, but less activity is difficult for me. Hard for me to stay with the writer.

I should schedule things in a way that is organic, where the manager is helping the artist. For example, after a session with a writing coach where I am stimulated and in a good mood, is the best time to take a walk, to process ideas. I need to pay attention to my moods and ways of being and cherish them, provide myself with more time with my thoughts. Of course, every day is different.

I like this lack of socializing. Preston said that every friendship, even at its best, is at the expense of interpsychic skills. There are always ways to improve our interpsychic skills, and we should prefer them over personal relations. Even our best relationships can be mutual disguising of deficiencies. Like the woman who marries because she can not support herself, or the man who marries the first woman he meets because he hates to be alone. However, in friendships one has the opportunity to advance oneself. In general, I am trying to gauge how much I use friendship in order to escape loneliness.

In some strange way that information may help me let go of my organizer. If I do that, I will trust the flow more.

Yesterday was the last seminar. Very worthwhile, reading, discussing, advancing spiritual health, couldn't be better. I sent a photo of the sunset after seminar.

Walking the dog
Meeting the morning at peace
Our sacred time

I forgot my book and money today when I went out. My supervisor is taking a break. Together we are working on how to relax and let the subconscious speak. The book and money were at the restaurant.

I realize that I and her feel safe here. Even Punchy was willing for me to acknowledge his part. Who knew the manager has a bodyguard ready for a fight if I get hurt? Trust the manager to be on top of his game. But all of us are transforming here in this seatown. She is secure, loving Baba, and now she is content and whole. She knows I listened, and she can be herself. I will not judge or ignore her. The organizer seems to be taking a vacation. Maybe he will make a great exception and start joining her on the beach, get some sun and rest, and just come back to work if we go to his town, New York.

And I, I am at peace with all these parts of me.

I still haven't cried enough but now I think those tears, the tears I need to cry, are not about her. She has spoken and there were no tears. She cried herself out in the Children's House. She has been held by me and is healed by my love.

But these tears in me that are blocked, and need to come out, are mine, and I must open that last door. I know this because I begin to feel the book is coming to an end. It is time. But suddenly she speak ups, "I am not ready, I am not willing to say goodbye or move on." She is holding on to me for dear life. She wants us to be together. And I feel the same. She is so dear to me.

She, too, knows there is something else.

A Grief Revealed

On Friday I could not write, she was clinging with full force. Maybe she feels we are moving on too fast. It was a lifetime of underground living and only a year of opening the wounds but is that enough?

Of course, this is not how I feel. We should move on because we always move forward. But I promised her we are keeping the door wide open anytime she has something to tell me. That is the change.

I call this apostocastisis. Preston referred to health as, "Instead of moving from damage to unhealthy guilt to depression, one chooses to move from concern to reparation and reconciliation."

I am a believer in second chances. We have no control over our first set of circumstances. The kibbutz separated my mother and me and left me on my own. I made good use of this void by building a life of giving support and being supported by Carlos, my friends, my writing and so much more.

But there is still one locked box left to open. I used to think the locked box was my mother's heart, but now I see it may have been my own. I locked it shut to keep my mother away since I was hurt. I wanted to open my heart to my little one, even though it took many years, but in the case of my mother, I did not want to risk opening it at all. I had my reasons.

I remember the last time I saw my mother. I had gone back to Israel when Elana told me my mother had lost a lot of weight and it looked like she has cancer. I had to decide, since we lived so far apart, when to go. I decided to go when we could still spend time together and talk. When I first walked in the door, she said, "We are not going to discuss my illness."

I accepted her wishes. I missed the opportunity to share with her how I was feeling about her and us after being away for so many years. I wasn't angry anymore and at that moment a lot of time had passed and I had been able to build a life I felt good about. So why didn't I tell her what I was feeling? We had spoken a lot in the past about our teaching. She had given me a lot of support in that area. But we did not share our yearnings, deeper thoughts, ever. It was my mother's decision to not come near her emotions. We spoke about functioning and performance. My manager learned a lot from her. But what did I want to tell her? That I loved her, that her joy and happiness were important to me. That I understood her sadness about her family in Poland and it touched me deeply. How talented she was with her knitting and crocheting, her dedication to her work which made it almost an art. How I admired her writing of poetry which showed her deep love for her family, nature, and a profound gratitude and guilt to have survived.

Eventually it came the time when I had to return to New York and I didn't want to say goodbye, knowing this would be the last time we would see each other. She walked to the door, we parted with light kisses. She was so sick and made a supreme effort to get up to see me leaving. She had her standards, pride in how things should be. The good qualities of the manager.

saying goodbye
we both stood at the door
touching eternity.

After we said goodbye, I then went with my brother to talk to the doctors in Haifa. I asked the doctor how much time she had left, and they could not commit. I was doing this in the hope I could stay longer. I took the train back to Tel Aviv, and I just sat there for two hours without moving, frozen by the realization of my final separation from my mother. We both knew we would never see each other again. We spoke a few more times on the phone and then Orna (my sister-in-law) called and said she had twenty-four hours to live. That was two weeks after my visit.

I gasped when I heard. As much as I knew she was dying, it was still a blow. I did not return for the funeral. I was heart-broken. She used to say, "I will never go back to Poland. I have no desire to go back." She expressed her disgust at the anti Semitism she had experienced there. But I felt she had now gone home to the famly she had lost. That was where she wanted to be.

Even today, it is hard for me to say outloud to her, "I love you so much. I had to go so far away from you to find my own life. It was a punishment for the separation and emotional estrangement that the kibbutz created, and I am sorry for that. It must have hurt you badly that I left, and brought back your old pain of leaving the burning house in Poland. I was angry and searching for a different, better life and, in the process, I hurt you a lot and you accepted it graciously. I learned from you a word is a word one keeps and one keeps one's promises. You taught me good values. The true value of money. What it delivers and what it doesn't. I never saw you cry. And your heart was crying all the time. Maybe that is why it is so hard for me to cry." So much to say.

Why did I never tell her any of that?

In traveling so far away to the States and redefining my life in the process, I didn't take the time to look and to understand – what my mother was carrying with her. I didn't give it any thought, busy surviving, but now I do and feel so much grief at how we did not really know each other.

My mother and I met often enough but we kept a distance. Even so, we felt a homesickness, one woman to the other. I am still homesick for her but, when she was ill, I had the feeling that her failing physical presence was not able to sustain the strength we both would need for me to go over the wall of intimacy. I felt I had the gear, the shoes, was physically well equipped to go over this wall, but I did not have the desire.

What do I think this wall is? Anger. When my mother said, "We are not going to talk about my illness," that reinforced the wall. There had been a wall between us for years that we could not bridge through communication. But I did not try to climb over it, as I have with others. Why? It was the resentment of her sacrificing me for the "greater good," the kibbutz and Israel. Of her susbtituting the home she left behind with the kibbutz, and not us.

Is it time to climb it now? I was always a climber. Many times, I dreamt of going up a steep hill. I like to climb, the process of climbing and challenges. I walk everywhere and find sharp hills, such as San Antonio in Peripolis, a seatown in Uruguay, where I walk up and up, only to arrive at a wide and almost spiritual panorama of the sea and the hills. I love the excitement and the exertion and strength it takes to go up and up.

With my mother, the time to have climbed that wall between us was when I said goodbye.

I learned two important lessons from my last trip to Israel. One is: memory is very subjective. I did not remember how beautiful and elegant my mother was and she was happy in the photos of Elana's wedding. Anger wipes everything out -- good and bad. It colors everything.

Even now, I would like to feel compassion for the suffering she went through, but I still feel the anger. Maybe it will melt now. But the anger protected me, helped me in life, acted as an agent for movement.

Funny how at the start of the book I was only aware of my own broken heart but, in the process, I have climbed the wall from my little one's side to my mother's side and begun to understand and identify with my mother's broken heart. Whenever I come close to it, I get so overwhelmed with sadness and tears about my lack of kindness. It is no longer about what she did not give me but what I exposed her to, another crucial separation.

Yesterday I was depressed with writing and came home and, as I was talking to Carlos, he was somewhat removed but there at the same time, and I quietly cried for both my mother and me. After I did that, the depression lifted. I love Carlos' light listening. He stays on the sideline,and I needed a touch of warmth, it was all I needed, his attentiveness. I told the experience to my sister and we spoke about the process of restoring my relationship to my mother. We can still make some reparation to my little one and to my mother. We can live a life my mother would be proud of. Elana and I can share joy with each other, we can live free of the burden she carried.

On our terrace
he just sat there and listened
gentle waves.

Cold inside and out
My heart and pen resisting
An empty page.

Again alone in Boca Chica, even the dog did not want
to stay at the sea, it was so cold. I decided to look the word
"compassion" up. Sympathetic, pity, concern for the suffering
and misfortune of others.

Gila says writing is better than therapy. And she is right.
Look at how I am able to go now to the root of things. Maybe
that is how you get to tenderness and love.

Morning in Punta
Harrowing winds pause
Ahead of dark news.

Punta is empty since it is winter. It is a time to think, feel,
and walk the dog at night when the buildings are dark. The
only light in our building is our apartment. It is lonely. "When
you love someone, you are lonely for him," Preston said. Was
I lonely for my mother? I missed her terribly as a baby. Could
not wait for her visits, to be in her holding arms, something I
want even today when I see people hugging. It touches me. I
love hugs. Carlos is a great hugger. It tells you so much about
the person, it is better than kisses. My mother was not a hugger,
not a physical person in any way shape or form. I saw her
naked body when she was in her last days, when trying to help
her take her shower, and she hid her body. I didn't feel warmth,
intimacy. Now I just want to sit next to her, hug her. She had
very nice hair which I would like to touch softly.

In my last visit, she was on morphine to ease her pain
and, she wanted her valium as well. I gave her the valium. It

reassured her. And while I sat next to her, the afternoon sun was penetrating near her window under the tree. The kibbutz was quiet, preparing for shabat. She lay in bed and her peacefulness spread through the room and united with the particles of light. And that light symbolized her acceptance. I remember she had a very developed sense of hearing and when people came to visit when she was ill and they were chatting in the next room, she commented how their conversation had nothing to do with visiting her. I think it hurt her feelings. I also remember being particularly stunned by her cabinet chest and the amount of medication she had when they cleared it after her death.

I am in Café Okay, which is not really the best for writing, but I had a good writing session. Maybe I am getting to hear my voice now after the discovery of how my mother affected my life. Gila and I exchange notes about parting with our parents, she from her father and me from my mother and we both knew it was the last time we would see them. It is such a powerful experience. Gila told me her father thanked her for her care and even joked with her. My mother's and my words were few and far between. We did speak on the phone later that day which was nice, just a mundane call on daily stuff and my impending trip back home. I believe we had a few more calls but, after a few days, they stopped too.

On my next trip to Israel, I visited her grave. I stood there and an overwhelming feeling of her relief came over me. She knew she left us in good shape. When a friend once commented she had very nice children, she answered, "I know," and she did. I keep coming back to her inner strength. I started writing my little one's memoir at the same age my mother died. We took different paths.

Hard to write with the sun outside being so strong; my eyes barely able to read or write. As I write, I realize that actually what is happening with my mother is I am saying goodbye to her now, which we were not able to do in person. My anger prevented me from suggesting to her in our last meeting that she should go and lie down, so she could be more comfortable and we could have a heart to heart chat. I was afraid I would become overwhelmed by my feelings of sadness. She too wanted to make it a brief departure without too many emotions. She is the one who came towards me to the door, as frail as she was. We could stand there and talk. It meant that the parting would be short. Understanding this experience will make me cry the millon tears Preston saw in my eyes. My tears are accessible for the first time and not buried deep inside. Opening this door will help me to love and part better with the people I care about, my family and my friends.

Preston believed my mother was afraid she would go mad, and pushed away her little girl, not embracing her own demons, her enemies. That is what happened to me in the concert when I wanted to run away, instead of befriending those feelings.

When Serena Williams lost in the US Open which was a very big deal for her, one of the commentators said she did not embrace how she felt and what it meant to her. She acted as if losing was okay and it cost her the tournament. She disowned her feelings.

My mother survived by disowning her past. It was too difficult, I understand but, in the process of doing so, she shut down her feelings completely.

Maybe the way I never spoke about my past with Carlos is because she was so silent about her past. When he introduced his group of friends to me, he was concerned we would not connect. We are so different about it. My past is behind me, his past is a source of his strength and memories. Always telling stories of his past. I live more for the future, forward looking. His best days were in his protected childhood, his family practically owned the neighborhood, and they were safe and happy.

Ah, now I can I feel tears all around me, the tears are coming, those tears I have wanted and needed to cry. When I think of what we missed together. A lot. Gila has some of my mother's best parts, like the love of poetry and reading, her intellectual approach and high moral standards. Things to explore.

I walked and exercised hard. Tired. Am in a different café, Café Okay, on the couch, at a smaller table, and it feels good. Preston talked of the importance of small talk, a way to connect superficially, which has value. I hear the Uruguayans talking. They love to chat.

> Sound of chopping
> Beginning of a nice day
> Is she crying?

I had a good writing session, and am getting more and more in touch with the depth of my feelings about my mother. All she lost. It is beyond my imagination that my mother could not land in Israel when the boat arrived. She was sent away to Lebanon, and came from Lebanon by train. And then she came to Eilon, a hard land of rocks and a wild landscape and tried to build a new life there. And the sense of purpose and commitment to Israel may have helped her grieving by giving her life meaning.

She could not go back. How she must have missed them. How many times she must have lay down and seen them. Did she say goodbye to them and how did she part with them the last time? Did she know it was the last time? She had to push it back. And she could in Israel -- they were so busy building the kibbutz and very tired physically. A great way to ignore grief. Mothering, too, I believe, gave her joy, even though it was intermittent.

A friend asked if my mother loved me. I didn't answer. "Sara, it's a very simple answer, yes or no."

"I don't know. She never said she did. Maybe she loved me. She loved the warrior in me."

My sister said yesterday she remembers my mother's love and warmth speaking about me. She is sure she loved me. But did I love her back?

My mother did not know me. She was so afraid, and that fear translated to me. She imagined the worst about me. She thought I drank too much and I was running and exercising too much. I was so shocked by what she thought of me.

Soothing the aching soul
The warmth and glare of the sun
Unimaginable pain.

I feel tremendous sadness and part of that may be my mother's. My little one felt her as well and was crying for her. And also a lot of that sadness is about my having mixed feelings. In retrospect, all the gas explosion entries and the burning skin has something to do with my mother, she who left a burning house.

Rachel mentioned she had compassion for both her parents. They had shared with her their hardships so she could identify with them. My mother never once spoke one word. She only told us her parent's names and that is all I ever remember. I didn't even know she had a niece. As I walked, I had this beautiful fantasy:

far in the horizon
the sunlight kisses and bathes her
bubbles of light.

My sister says my going into this pain is already benefiting the family. I have much more love, as a result of my book.

The soup is great and warm, perfect for a grey winter day with the mandolin music in the background. I switched back to Boca Chica, much more effective for my needs. My little one is also feeling the sadness penetrating her little body's bones and cells. She does not know who she is crying over. It's interesting that when I straightened out my relationship with her, let her say her piece and gave her a permanent voice in my life, my mother appeared, and it is her grief taking over me.

At first it was just me trying to understand and forgive, but my little one is so eager to be included. She let me know how much she loved my mother and how they spent time together secretly, watching each other's back. My mother truly loved her and even laughed with her. It was the time my mother had fun. They both kept it very quiet.

My little one lives in the moment and with her feelings. Maybe she was not as angry as I was. It is me she doesn't want to let go of. She has more expectations of me. I didn't take care of the child in me well enough, so she has more gripes with me than my mother. My manager is around but lower key. He still shows up every morning when I sit down to write but he is much less bossy. He does his job and leaves. He insists less, he knows his place and feels good about it. No doubt my relationship with my little one has affected my relationships all over, with Carlos, family and friends. Rachel said her daughter in law gets up every day and thinks, What mitzvah can I do today? I love it. I don't think it outloud but unconsciously.

Today is the end of the month, and I finalized the numbers with Mark, my accountant, walked Poppy who was eager to come. I love when Carlos and I are close. The air is different, there is tenderness in the air which is when I love being home.

It is white and quiet
the chopping in the kitchen
Café Okay.

I am in Café Okay and the rain is non-stop, the dog is a huge problem as he hates the rain. I have to look for a break to walk him. No one else is here which is great for writing. They lowered the music, it is not the music for writing. I learned that one can block off noise, but I am not sure how. Sitting on the couch, a home away from home, and the rain gives me privacy. I want to go back to what happened last Friday. I went to have a massage and I heard Elenora on the phone, animated. I asked her who she was talking to. She had bought her mother a phone so her mother could be in touch with her family whenever her mother felt lonely. It made me remember how much my mother wanted and needed things. How she wanted to decorate the house. My father did not want to spend the money and, when they finally got some new furniture, she was so happy. She didn't stand her ground with my father or me. She loved to bake, loved sweets, cookies, cakes. It was the only consolation to her, some sweetness in her life.

I felt so touched by how Elenora loves and takes care of her mother which I wish I had done. I wish I could have bought my mother the furniture she wanted to buy, the jewelry she so much loved. Her mouth was sealed, I never remember her asking for anything. I ended up cying at the massage, for what I didn't give her and I am looking for ways to grow from this missed opportunity.

In my dreams
I buy you a string of pearls
my little queen.

I don't want to feel that way about Carlos. I waited for the right moment on the way back home to tell him about my mother. He was in bed listening in the gentle way Carlos listens. I shared with him my regret about my mother and how I did not want to repeat what I did with my mother with him. He knows I am soon going to New York and, inspired by Elenora, I will buy him a phone with What's App so he can call whenever. I consider Carlos profound because he says very little. He takes it in and processes it. I cannot have the same regrets when he dies. He said, "I will survive your trip and furthermore this is a very short one." I have to stay in the here and now.

Elenora suggests that when I am in Israel, I should read part of my book to my mother at the cemetery. But even as I feel tenderly toward her, I still remember that, when we talked and there was an opening and I tried to take our discussion further, a door would slam shut in my face. How dare I dig? I was getting in the danger zone of forbidden memories. I who hate shut doors. I understand it better now, we couldn't go there.

this slightly open door
felt like an invitation
but slammed shut in my face.

It really marked me emotionally, how startled and unprepared I was for it, the lack of kindness. I feel the same way when Carlos cuts me short. It takes me back to that time.

I keep my mother's book by my bed. She wrote poetry in Hebrew. The book and I have a physical closeness she and I did not have. I can see that her language is rich. Her Hebrew is better than mine, she worked hard on it. She was very talented. She mentions and references prayers in her poetry. I had no idea about her religious roots. She named the first book, MO-DEANI, with a phrase from part of a prayer. She never talked about religion. It was Rachel who taught me about the siddur, the prayer book, and what to do in shul.

But what I find is that her book opens flood gates in me, and I sleep with it and carry it. I talk to Carlos and then walk in Punta crying at this missed closeness. That we didn't get to share —what we didn't have. The wall now is down, it came down when I identified with her sorrow, with what she went through. Her poems talk about Europe, about where she was born, our nation, the humiliation. It's all there, restrained in poetic language. And I am now, through this book, having a relationship I did not have with her.

Interestingly, my mother referred to herself in her poems as "she." I write about "her." I find new parallels in my emotion that echo hers, but we have to be detectives since her feelings are not so obvious.

And as I open up, I now am also remembering some of the good things. She was deeply serious and had an inner independence and I lived out that life for her. She admired my courage. Rachel and Mark came to visit the kibbutz, and Mark asked, "Was Sara persona non grata in the kibbutz?" My mother poked my father and then she nodded almost gleefully, "Did you hear what he asked?" Rachel took note that she took pleasure in the question. But it was not so simple. She admired my freedom but it also made her jealous. She was not able to roam the world like I was. She had a monkey on her back.

I see that my success in my life perhaps came from the unconscious desire to actualize the life my mother wished to have. She wanted a worldly writer/poet life with a principled strong value system. In some ways, I have a healthy version of her life. She did right but could not shake off her past. Who could? It would be an impossible task.

I hold them tight
her two books of poetry
the hugs we didn't share.

Feeling a little exhausted from the last two days and need time to recover. Lay low, not happy, not sad, just be. I am grateful for the book my father created in my mother's memory which I saw again in Israel. My mother wrote in Yiddish, but my father had a few of the letters translated. These are the most precious gems of this book. I am beginning to see first-hand parts of her I had no access to before reading her diary.

My mother wrote in 30/11/1940: *In Vilna, it's quiet and silent and warm inside. Carissa, Yanka and Devora went. I stayed alone. I am not sad at all. I expected that they would all leave. I felt like staying alone. Alone? No, I don't think so. While I am alone, I have someone close to me, near me and I am talking to him and listening. Sometimes the same phenomenon repeats itself. Maybe it's the pencil and the paper that I am writing on? These are my yearnings? No, these are only the instruments, not because of them I want to stay alone, they are just helping me to speak to someone else. With whom? I don't want to tell. It is not important. What is important is that my friends could leave so I could stay alone.*

8/12/40: *It seems that the fire called me: Come and sit next to me. Come closer and tell me about whatever you feel. I am listening to the voice of the fire. I take the chair and I sit next to the fire. In the first moment, she is very noisy, impatient, as if she wants to know everything, to scream, to shout, and to jump up and down. While I get closer and listen carefully to her shouting and to the noise, I find out that this screaming is directed towards me and I should get closer. I listen to the fire inside and I want to tell something that is very sad and difficult. That I have a strange feeling of being disturbed and anxous. It doesn't let me sit in one place; the fire loses patience. Most likely, she doesn't like when someone is sad and unhappy. Stupid, the fire said all of a sudden. In order for me to listen with more attention, the fire sent a spark that touched my hand with pain. Stupid, why are you sitting in the room alone? Why aren't you joining the other people? This is not good. Your place is not in this room in between the walls. Get up and join everyone else, be with them. I feel shame toward the fire. I know she is right, but I don't listen to her and I stay where I am in my place.*

28/12/1940: *My friend Sarale was here and she left. She is happy with Itzak, her boyfriend. I was happy to hear it. It took a very short time to get ALL THE INFORMATION. But what is all the information? she asked. I know so little about her and I told her very little about myself. Is it going to make our lives better that there is no time to talk about everything? The happenings of the days and times are proceding at a very fast rate. Months come and go, and they push*

*away the happenings of yesterday. They ask, Is what
happened yesterday important? Here we are young, new,
we need a solution. News is the problem of the day. We
don't want to spend time with the news. Yesterday I got
regards from my mother, father, all the relatives so I am
not alone. I am with them together. I feel good when
I am with them, regards that Sarale brought me from
my home.*

I took a new seat at Café Okay. It is good to change places.
I see glimpses of myself in my mother's writing which is a surprise. As an example, we both have a need to stay alone. Why
do I prefer to be apart, or outside of places and things, looking
in? The outsider. The answer surprised me. The kibbutz was
such a communal place, and I love to interact and exchange
but only on my own and not full time. Even in marriage, I love
the coming and going.

> walking between trees and gardens
> in shadows of smoke and burn
> her heavy steps.

But I see that she loved me when I read the inscription to
me in her book: Dearest Sara, the separation and the longing
for you that gathered in my heart finds words in ways gathered
in the pages of this book. Yours with lots of love,
  Twenty years she and I lived apart and in different coun-
tries and could not speak. And now we do through our books.

> my sweet breakfast
> a bowl of singing fruits
> and a cup of coffee.

Winnicott said, Creativity is the ability to surprise your-self. Creativity is the engine of life. And my mother too used that engine with her poems. I don't have her book of poems with me today. It is by my bed. I keep on reading them. I don't think I can translate them. The vocabulary is so extensive I don't think I can do it and, even though her language is poetic, her emotions are hidden. I am so glad she felt the urge to write before her death, to give voice to the family she left behind. She honored them. She wrote of them and her profound love of nature.

Heard from Kat yesterday about her condition that she should walk as little as possible. She mentioned in her email how she is going to manage to see the trees in Central Park, by resting on the benches in between her walk. When I told Carlos, I broke out sobbing. We have to have nature in our lives, it gives us hope and courage. It is what sustained my mother, the Eilon valley sunset. The beauty of Eilon helped her stay away from her unimaginable memories, and played a major role in keeping her sane. What we love weaves us to-gether and sustains us.

But her own beauty, she stayed distant from, except for writing. It touched me when I heard her voice. My father too had a nice voice and Carlos does also and sings his love affair with tangos. Shortly before my father died, we celebrated Rosh Hashanah and we sang together. His memory was incoherent at that stage, but his singing – the words and the melody -- perfect.

My sister, Elana, does not remember her own final sepa-ration with Ima. It was not as specific as mine because I came from far away and had to leave. Elana does have memories of being physically close with Ima, lying in bed with her (never happened to me.) She remembers that Ima had a lot of complaints, upset about our father and more. Glad I didn't have to hear it. She acted as a victim in her marriage and in the kibbutz.

Elana became closer to my parents when they were older, after I left. My father lived for 19 years alone after my mother's death. He talked to Elena daily about his joys and sorrows, his pain and aches, his cooking and his grandchildren. He saved pennies in order to give each grandchild one year in college. His grandchildren used to stop by his house on the way to their home for sweets. He always had a full house of treats. On one of my visits, we went to a restaurant together and we were looking for a place to have dessert afterwards. "No," my father said," come to my house. I will treat you to the best dessert there is." And, indeed, we went back home and he set up a table with all kinds of goodies, chocolates, nuts, tea and coffee and cakes, and such variety. He had a love of hospitality, in particular with a family he trusted. David took such good care of my parents and my father had such admiration for him. Elana gave them their first granddaughter.

I love when I speak with Carlos and he says how grateful he is for this life he has. "Oh Sara, I am going to go now to my bed. My electric blanket is on and I have the newspaper and I am so grateful for all I have." It warms the heart. We are home to each other and I created a home for him.

Today Carlos went with the dog to Montevideo. I am by myself in Punta. Usually, we are always together here. Gila talked about how the Vietnamese Buddhists call their spouse, "their home." It is how I feel about my marriage. It's not one where we walk day and night holding hands. We are there for each other in the background, creating a safe place to start from, and go to pursue our dreams and inspiration, a safe place to come back to from the adventures of the world and life. As

Barbara Walters said, If she went on a long trip away to Africa, she had her husband to call to say she had arrived. Someone on the other end who cares. But we also have space between us, which is why I so admire how the Japanese live. They know how to create space in close proximity.

I feel much more in my body. I am healing…my head worked overtime all my life. Now it is time for more joy and less involvement with my head who had to compensate for my own and my mother's losses. I feel the end of my book is near. Still grieving for Ima. Still missing the contact and many more tears are there but now I know they will come out. That is what the book did for me, it was so buried and now I trust that whatever needs to come out, will come out.

In Boca Chica which is a better place than Café Okay. I like the friendliness and the good service. Friendliness is very important to me; the kibbutz was not friendly. We were to-gether 24 hours without a healthy distance. I remember how struck Carlos was by how people did not say good morning to each other when he visited the kibbutz. This proximity made havoc with human interaction, like ships passing in the night.

I went to Montevideo and I met a friend, Patricia, an artist bohemian person who is the curator of the Spanish Cultural Institute here. She lived in New York for 4 years on a Fulbright scholarship. She told us how great Montevideo is. I believe her, and want to go back there and experience Montevideo from her perspective, the creativity. There is a great culture in Montevideo.

Came back to a long cold morning walk.
long red beaks
bathing in the beaches of Punta
cold day.

Mother Theresa was made a saint yesterday. I was moved by her doubts if she loved God enough, if she had given all of herself. All of us always have doubts, questions lingering. There are no limits to how much one can love, and how deep. In my life I feel no matter how much I love my husband, friends, family, I could always do more, understand them better, listen better. Can I ever feel I completely exhausted my ability to love? The answer is no. The other day I spoke with one of my adopted daughters and we just chatted and I felt such deep deep love for her for no apparent reason. It was new to have this intense feeling. There is a sea of love and one has to tap into it.

It is raining cats and dogs, grey but, in my soul, the light is on. She is happy. I walked today in the cold in my lovely Punta, one of the few people on the Brava side but it adds a vigor to walk bundled up.

> Scarf hat and gloves
> battling the waves and winds
> alone and free.

I woke up and my spirit is up. The spirit is ageless. Again, gray day with hope for a sunny afternoon. I am starting with hopefully new habits. No iphone before bedtime and try to read. Wonderful books are my highest value; what I aspire to but don't get around to. My strongest value is the iphone and politics. Self respect comes from doing one's highest values. That is why it is best to do the most difficult thing at first and then you ride on your self respect the rest of the day.

Ann mentioned in seminar yesterday that Hafiz speaks of dancing. How one can increase light in one's life by living in one's heart, doing what one loves with people one loves.

Choosing love all the time rather than anger, jealousy or any other bad feeling that comes up. It is a choice.

> She wanted a muffin
> I listen and gave it to her
> Harmony, joy.

After the US election, it feels like September 11 all over again. Could hardly get myself out of bed. I walked to relieve the pain. God only knows what's going to happen. He is so ill equipped to lead, vindictive. Hillary is an insider and people wanted a change more than anything. My only consolation is how we can make good use of it. Carlos and I are not at peace. He gets intolerant when I am in a bad mood. I am thinking I will maybe go to New York. It is amazing how when my heart is broken, my manager steps in so quickly and takes over. My manager has a direct line to my heart and my broken parts. He is the one, Let's get into action, not wallow in conflict. Take a first step and then the next one. It is not a bad control, his stepping in.

> Slow walking steps
> fog engulfed my heart
> not even a half smile.

The effect of the election is there but wearing off some. Less intensity and we will see what is to come. Maybe there will be surprises. I want to be an observer, as the Zen book proposes, of the feelings and the drama, not caught up in the hysteria. I welcome that approach when things are loaded and out of my control. To be in the experience, not be in the opinions which the writer calls false suffering. Love that notion. Maybe all suffering is false suffering.

Today as I walked my dog, exercised, shopped in the supermarket, I could hear her voice. It's the different rhythm of here. We are co-operating together. It is a brand new beginning, living in the here and now, reading about how fear is going to the suffering of the past, to the familiar, or to the future. Our fear that what we have might be taken away from us. We lose the moment. I got this emphasis in seminar, and want to make it into a habit. It was a small seminar but I got a lot out of it, put a lot into it.

We might move from Punta which makes me sad. Punta that I love, the beauty, the sea that hugs her all around with stretched arms. But Punta does not brag about her beauty. She wears it quietly and leaves it to her visitors to discover. Her sunsets wash the buildings all around with magical light and a glow that lasts way after the sun disappears. A Uruguayan professor was asked, "Why did you come back to Uruguay?" "For the light," he answered. Is it Uruguay's geographic proximity to the end of the world? Being all the way down south? I love the people here too, sweet, on their own time, not the speed of New York city time. They seem to not be tempted by money. What they want is to have a home, have a matte, share asado with friends, watch soccer games; these are the real pleasures of life. And I suspect they know much more about that than I do. I have learned a lot here, to sit with my book every morning, to listen and write, to have lunch on our terrace with Carlos, to walk my dog to the sea every morning.

It is all about taking one step at a time. When A. Olman's body shut down in the third part of the Iron Man, which he took on after his lung collapsed, he said just talking to himself to encourage his body to run did not work. The body could not comprehend the whole picture. To think of the whole distance of the 42 km terrified his body. But he could take small steps. After a person helped him put on his running shoes, he just focused on the 1 ½ km where there was a station and he could get some water. After this one, he felt better and proceded to go on. He finished the race, the power of small steps.

Baba told me how hard it is for him to pick me up when I return from New York, to drive when it is dark. But he wakes up, gets into the car, drives the silent highway in the very early morning, and there he is. Barbara Corcoran says she doesn't like exercise, but places the sneakers near her bed and, in the morning, on her feet, takes the first step and the rest follows. This is how we build.

Two nights ago we got a call from Judy that Alberto, Carlos' old friend, died. It made us both sad. The two men used to watch football matches together. Baba lay in bed and sobbed. I never saw this. I worry for her being alone in Milford but at least she has her work. This loss touched Baba's heart, the proximity to the end of his own life as well. I sat next to him without words, just engulfed with sadness. I love Baba for how in touch he is with his feelings. I wrote to his two sons in New York and both responded with deep humanity. I love them.

a call came late
he exited quietly
no trace, just memory.

Yet life goes on. I take my walks with the dog. I work on my book. I keep in mind that love is the way of life. As an example, I was a bit annoyed with Carlos, but I brought the newspaper up to him and brought his pill and a glass of juice. Just the act of giving these to him changed my feelings.

Christmas is over. We celebrated quietly with well-cooked food. Carlos was in good spirits, he had a few drinks which always brings him joy. What a blessing. The day after, I slept while it was raining hard, stayed home resting. I could almost not control the tiredness at the party. The weather helped me to rest since I cannot walk in the rain. Then Carlos wanted me to come to his bed. I did not feel like it, but I did it and, after, it changed the feeling to peace and intimacy.

Later, I decided to sit outside, when the weather cleared. Read through Rachel and Kathy's book of Preston's writing. He said, "The spirit transcends time; it is not concerned with temporal time, but with eternal time, which intervenes in temporal time; an example is the beauty expressed in music, dance, and art." I would add to that when you do for others, you are living in eternal time. And when you are your truest self, you are in eternal time. But I would really say that we are in eternal time when we are wholly present. With our little one and ourselves and the sea of forgiveness and the recurring waves of love.

The storm has passed
On the silent shores of Punta
Eternal blue skies.

About the Author

Sara Gelbard is a woman of three homes – Israel, New York, and Punta del Este in Uruguay. This may be because she never had a home. She was born in one of the first Israeli kibbutzim in Western Galil near the Lebanon border, of Polish parents who escaped the tremendous horror of Europe. They escaped, but their families did not, and consequently, their commitment to the kibbutz was ideological, necessary, and fueled by a broken heart.

The first kibbutzim were the most stringent in their rules – mothers only allowed in at feeding times – and 24 children in each Children's House, with only one circulating guardian at night. The children were taught to be little soldiers, and performed their duties, and needs and emotions were discouraged. For a sensitive individualistic person, like Sara, this became a burden that would later haunt her. She excelled in the kibbutz, in the Israeli army (in her case, becoming a Navy officer), at a Tel Aviv Movement and Dance School, and teaching at the College of Sde Boker (where Ben Gurion lived.) She excelled but carried a tremendous loneliness and sadness of having lived without real connection or having been given the gift of self-expression. The army offered more self-expression than the kibbutz. Even with her excelling at the kibbutz, she was denied by them her second year of college, because they deemed her too independent. With that, she left.

After the Six Day War, when all Israel was celebrating, Sara decided to enroll in the Martha Graham Dance School and moved to New York. There she went through the struggles of an immigrant with language, finding work, although she was helped by a dear friend also from Israel, and by a philosophical psychoanalyst who ran seminars on the interior life. This saved her and opened the inner life to her. She got her BA in Economics from Fordham, became a successful real estate broker, selling homes to others, which was a form of reparation. She married her Uruguayan husband (then in New York) who became her first "home."

At seventy, she was walking in the beautiful Punta del Este, with its ocean on two sides, and that little girl's voice, who never could be heard, or speak of what she felt, bubbled up. THE SOUND OF HER VOICE is Sara's exploration of what it was like to live in this unfeeling world as a child, the healing in writing, what her three homes are to her, how marriage healed her, and, ultimately, how she came to understand and forgive how her mother could, in her way, give her away. Sara sprinkles her book with haikus that go to the heart of such a journey. The entire book speaks to all of us who have a voice inside us that must be listened to if we want to open our hearts.